THE CENTENARY
OF
MOUNT HOLYOKE COLLEGE

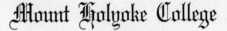

Mount Holyoke College

1837   *1937*

SEMINARY BUILDING.
Opened in 1837, Destroyed by fire, 1896.

IN the year of our Lord eighteen hundred and thirty-six, an institution for the higher education of women was chartered, and its doors opened to students in November, eighteen hundred and thirty-seven. Situated in the village of South Hadley, on the genial soil of the Connecticut Valley, where the river bends to the southeast under the shadow of Mount Holyoke, it took its name from that eminence, and was called Mount Holyoke Female Seminary

The new institution owed its existence to the vision and courage of Mary Lyon. Honouring, as she did, the untrammelled human mind, she laboured all her life to bring to young women the joy of healthy mental activity. She believed that a woman's seminary could be permanent, continuing onward in its operations from generation to generation. That her faith was justified has been due in great part to the loyalty of friends who have helped the College to weather its periods of difficulty and incertitude Other institutions, themselves struggling for existence in those early years, have been generous with encouragement; and miniature models of Mount Holyoke in several lands have grown to noble proportions

IN this present year nineteen hundred and thirty-seven, Mount Holyoke College proposes to celebrate its one hundredth anniversary, not only to honour its founder and with her the generous donors who made possible her dream, but to commemorate and renew her pledge It was in the month of May, eighteen hundred and thirty-eight, that the original building was dedicated. It will be in the month of May, on the seventh and eighth days, that our ceremonies will take place.

The old foursquare hall in which Mary Lyon taught has long since given place to the Gothic structures of the modern college. But the youth that moves among them is as inspiring as it was to her, the New England spring will open before our eyes as it did before hers; and we can together lift up our hearts to the same encircling hills which so constantly renewed her faith and hope for the future.

Therefore, when the rigours of the winter season shall be well overpast, we hope that you may join with us in celebrating the centenary of our College. We shall welcome, personally and for your sake, any representative whom you may send

Facsimile of the Preliminary Invitation (9 x 11) to the Centenary

THE CENTENARY

of

MOUNT HOLYOKE COLLEGE

Friday and Saturday
May Seventh and Eighth
Nineteen Hundred and Thirty-Seven

PUBLISHED BY THE COLLEGE
SOUTH HADLEY, MASSACHUSETTS
1937

GEORGE BANTA PUBLISHING COMPANY, MENASHA, WISCONSIN

DEDICATED TO
MOUNT HOLYOKE'S 17,472 DAUGHTERS
OF THE FIRST CENTURY

TABLE OF CONTENTS

SUPPLEMENT

APPENDIX

LIST OF ILLUSTRATIONS

CHRONOLOGY

THE CHARTERS

Mount Holyoke Female Seminary	1836
Mount Holyoke Seminary and College	1888
Mount Holyoke College	1893

PRINCIPALS AND PRESIDENTS

		Number of Years
Mary Lyon, Founder	1837–1849	12
Mary C. Whitman Mary W. Chapin Helen M. French } * Julia E. Ward Elizabeth Blanchard	1849–1890	41
Elizabeth Storrs Mead	1890–1900	10
Mary Emma Woolley	1900–1937	<u>37</u> 100

President Woolley's retirement in June, 1937
ends the first century

The second century begins

Roswell Gray Ham	1937–

---

* Besides these five principals of the middle years, there were two acting heads, Sophia D. Hazen Stoddard and Louise F. Cowles, and an elected President, Mary A. Brigham, who did not live to serve.

FOREWORD

"A HUNDRED years of higher education for women" is naturally an exciting subject to women whose own education, like that of Henry Adams, has covered a considerable part of the century. To college students of these later years the phrase has often sounded artificial—an attempt to evoke an emotion about something as everyday as one's bread and butter and orange juice. Yet something of the old excitement rose once more in the atmosphere of Mount Holyoke College, like a keen wind blowing, a few months before 1937 dawned.

The election of a new president, to take office a year later, focused the attention of the College, of the alumnae, of the English-speaking world, for at least an enlightening moment, on the contemporary record of educated women. The final year of the first hundred, and the final year of an unbroken succession of women principals and presidents, became an unexpectedly stimulating time, in an unexpectedly conspicuous place, for the celebration recorded in this book.

And so the background of the Centenary Celebrations held lively ideas about Mount Holyoke and its founder, about the claims of women to shape their own intellectual destiny, about the obligations resting upon those who are carrying a woman's college into its second century. Different readers will bring to this account very diverse views of the events surrounding the particular moment in Mount Holyoke's history during which the celebration was held. But every reader will see that the light and warmth of fresh excitement contributed to the occasion a vitality that recreated something of the spirit in which Mount Holyoke was founded a hundred years ago.

EVENTS OF FRIDAY
MAY THE SEVENTH

FORERUNNERS

FOR many weeks before the Centennial there had been an unwonted stir about the campus; something clearly was in the air. Lawns were trimmed, gardens were set in order, tall poles appeared at every entrance, lamps could be found in trees and other hidden places. At last the stage was completely set, and on the night of May the sixth suddenly the clock in Mary Lyon Hall shone blue among the tree tops; soft lights flooded Gothic doorways and towers; Lower Lake glowed in a magic of silver and blue. On the morning of May the seventh silver pennants with blue numerals 1837, 1937 hung from all the silver poles. South of Student-Alumnae Hall had arisen a huge tent, big enough to stir gay circus sentiments, big enough to cover assembled alumnae. East of Skinner Hall chairs had been set to accommodate five thousand guests; facing these was a garlanded platform on either side of which hung great silver and blue banners bearing proudly the seals of Mount Holyoke's five Daughter Colleges. All of this, together with the enchantment of early May, its drifts of dogwood, its abundant forsythia and bright Japanese quince, made the college grounds a gracious setting for the festival that was to celebrate the close of Mount Holyoke's first hundred years.

STUDENT FROLIC

At seven o'clock on Friday morning the Campus awoke to the sound of trumpet and bagpipes played by kiltie-clad Scotch pipers who led the way to the Student Frolic, official opening of the Centenary Celebration.

Several hundred undergraduates and early-rising guests followed to the North Campus which became a gay scene of activity centering in three Maypoles, each surmounted by the waving pennant of one of our three American Daughter Colleges.

Twenty-four students dancing about each pole to the music of the bagpipes gayly wound in and out varying the intricate designs made by the intertwining streamers of Mount Holyoke blue and the green, gold, and blue of the Daughter Colleges. Standing beside each pole, in company with a Mount Holyoke student, and bearing a miniature pole presented as a part of the ceremony, was a student representative of one of these colleges, Edith Drake from Western, Jean Fawcett from Lake Erie, and Jane Taylor from Mills.

At intervals there was singing in honor of the Daughters, led by Katherine Swenarton, student Song Leader. A climax to the Frolic was reached when a group of laughing seniors energetically skipped rope about the poles, reviving an old Mount Holyoke custom.

Eight o'clock found students and guests returning to the residence halls for a festive breakfast including strawberries and cream and other delicacies. At her place each student found a boutonniere of forget-me-nots with silver leaves provided by the Community organizations. The boutonniere was the distinguishing badge of a student in Mount Holyoke's Centennial Celebration.

CENTENARY SERVICE OF COMMEMORATION

Close upon the light-hearted frolic of the present generation of undergraduates came the more serious memorial services for the students and scholars and leaders of the past. At nine o'clock in Mary Lyon Chapel was held the Centenary Service of Commemoration, conducted by the Reverend David E. Adams, D.D., Professor of the History and Literature of Religion. Dr. Adams had prepared the order of worship and had written the prayers, which were used with the responses from the Vesper Service, familiar to all lovers of Mount Holyoke. The Senior Class was present in cap and gown; and music was provided by the Senior Choir directed by Miss Ruth Douglass, with Miss Clara Tillinghast at the organ. At the close of the litany, the entire congregation adjourned to the Grove, where representatives of the Senior Class decorated the grave of Mary Lyon. Prayer was offered by Dr. Frederick Harlan Page, whose mother, Lucy Barnard, was a member of the first class at Mount Holyoke.

ORDER OF SERVICE

ORGAN PRELUDE, Largo.................................. *Handel*

PROCESSIONAL HYMN, Our God, Our Help in Ages Past...... *Croft*

CALL TO WORSHIP (*The Congregation seated*)

INVOCATION AND LORD'S PRAYER WITH RESPONSE

RESPONSIVE READING (*The Congregation standing*)

> Seek ye the Lord while he may be found;
> Call ye upon him while he is near:
>
> *Let the wicked forsake his way,*
> *And the unrighteous man his thoughts;*
>
> And let him return unto the Lord, and he will have mercy upon him;
>
> *And to our God, for he will abundantly pardon.*
>
> For my thoughts are not your thoughts,
> Neither are your ways my ways, saith the Lord.
>
> *For as the heavens are higher than the earth,*
> *So are my ways higher than your ways,*
> *And my thoughts than your thoughts.*
>
> For as the rain cometh down and the snow from heaven,
> And returneth not thither, but watereth the earth,
>
> *And maketh it bring forth and bud*
> *And give seed to the sower and bread to the eater,—*
>
> So shall my word be that goeth forth out of my mouth;
> It shall not return unto me void,

But it shall accomplish that which I please
And it shall prosper in the thing whereto I sent it.

For ye shall go out with joy and be led forth with peace:

The mountains and the hills shall break forth before you into singing,
And all the trees of the field shall clap their hands.

Instead of the thorn shall come up the fir tree,
And instead of the brier shall come up the myrtle tree;

AND IT SHALL BE TO THE LORD FOR A NAME,
FOR AN EVERLASTING SIGN THAT SHALL NOT BE CUT OFF.

GLORIA PATRI

ANTHEM, The Countless Host..................................*Grieg*

SCRIPTURE LESSON

HYMN...*Tune, Old Hundred*

Sung at the Dedication of Mount Holyoke Female Seminary, May 3, 1838

> Almighty, from Thy glorious throne,
> O look in gentle kindness down,
> While here we come, with reverence meet
> To lay our offering at Thy feet.
>
> Thy guiding finger, Lord, we trace
> That chose for us this lovely place;
> And bade this house securely stand
> Cradled amid a mountain band.
>
> Where mingling charms attraction lend,
> And nature's rarest beauties blend.
> All was the work of Thy design;
> The beauteous fabric, Lord, is Thine.
>
> This hall so spacious and so neat,
> Where young rejoicing spirits meet
> The intellectual wreath to twine,
> God of eternal power, is Thine.
>
> We give Thee all—we yield to Heaven
> The boon Thy gracious hand has given.

And yet for all Thy goodness shown
Naught can we give Thee but Thine own.

Now Father let this cherished spot
Be in Thy counsels ne'er forgot.
Here let Thy holiest influence rest,
And rule in every youthful breast.

By Sarah H. Browne, Class of 1840

LITANY OF COMMEMORATION (*The Congregation seated*)

Congregation: Almighty and Everlasting God, before whom stand the spirits of the living and the dead; Light of lights; Fountain of wisdom and goodness; who livest in all pure and humble and gracious souls: for her who in years past dreamed a dream, and toiled for its fulfillment; who laid lasting foundations, and built well upon them; who gave unstintingly of strength and love and labor till her years were ended; who lives on in the grateful memory of the following generations—

Choir: We give Thee thanks and praise through Jesus Christ our Lord.

Congregation: For all who have followed her, carrying on the noble tradition of great leadership in this College; who have built their lives into the years of its growth; who have planned and toiled and sacrificed that the young women of America and of the world might find the way to a more abundant life; who have labored that generations yet to come might enter in to their labor—

Choir: We render thanks unto Thee, Thou giver of every good and perfect gift, through Jesus Christ our Lord.

Congregation: For all who through the years have given their lives to the teaching of youth in this College; who, dedicated to sound scholarship and true learning, have laid the foundations for progress and achievement in many lives; who by the example of faithful and devoted service have inspired with truth and beauty those who looked to them for guidance; whose faithfulness and devotion are an inseparable part of our present heritage—

Choir: We bless Thy grace in Jesus Christ our Lord.

Congregation: For the thronging thousands of young women whose feet have sought this hilltop for a hundred years in the quest for knowledge and for life abundant; whose eager dreams and earnest strivings have been woven irrevocably into the living spirit of this institution; who have gone forth to carry its message and its power and its ideals to the uttermost ends of the earth, whose lives bear witness to its beauty and its strength, we give Thee thanks and praise this day.

And we pray for all who today are entering in to this goodly heritage, that they may not fail nor falter, but in loyalty to great traditions and in realization of a great opportunity, may be worthy of all who have gone before.

Choir: Hear Thou our prayer and answer all our petitions, by granting us Thy spirit, through Jesus Christ our Lord.

Congregation: And now for all who have seen and understood the dream of the Founder, and have undergirded this College with the gifts which have made possible its work, strengthened the hands of its leaders, empowered the labors of its teachers, and reared structures of brick and stone for the abiding place of its enduring spirit, we offer thanks and praise.

Choir: Amen.

Congregation: For state and nation under the protection of whose laws and by the favor of whose nurture from the beginning this College has dwelt in security and peace in the beauty of this place, we offer thanks and praise.

Choir: Amen.

Congregation: Sanctify the ties that bind us to the Unseen, that we may hold the dead in continued remembrance, that the blessing of their fidelity and fortitude may rest upon us, that with cleansed hearts and strengthened wills, we may walk with humble steps the way that leadeth unto life. We beseech Thee to hear us, O Lord.

Choir: Amen.

Congregation: In the communion of all saints, the redeemed of all ages, and our blessed dead who dwell at home with Thee, in the fellowship of Thy whole family in earth and heaven, we render thanksgiving and glory unto the Lord our God, through Jesus Christ our Saviour.

Choir: Amen.

RECESSIONAL HYMN, For All the Saints . . . . . . *Barnby*

ORGAN POSTLUDE, Saint Anne's Fugue. . . . . *Bach*

COMMEMORATION PRAYER by the REVEREND FREDERICK HARLAN PAGE

BENEDICTION by the REVEREND HENRY DAVID GRAY

ALUMNAE SYMPOSIUM

Guests, faculty, and students walked from the exercises in the Grove to the Alumnae Symposium in Chapin Auditorium in the midst of a sudden downpour. The gay umbrellas provided a note of color in welcome contrast to the lowering clouds above them. The Alumnae Symposium opened at ten-thirty o'clock, Mrs. Maude Titus White, President of the Alumnae Association, presiding.

MRS. WHITE: Mount Holyoke College is celebrating the completion of one hundred years of continuous education of women on this campus. We are gathered to honor the founder, Mary Lyon, her successors, and particularly Mary E. Woolley. Their ideas and their ideals have reached a rich fruition in the Mount Holyoke College of 1937. On this foundation we build our future. Their ideas and ideals will continue to develop and endure.

As President of the Mount Holyoke College Alumnae Association, I welcome you this morning to our Centennial Celebration, and I think this weather is just a challenge to the Mount Holyoke spirit.

The invocation will be given by Dr. Mary Ely Lyman, Lecturer in English Bible at Union Theological Seminary, and Lecturer in Religion at Barnard College. Dr. Lyman.

INVOCATION

Let us pray. Oh, God, before whose face the generations rise and pass away, Thou hast been our dwelling place in all generations, before the mountains were brought forth or before Thou hadst formed the earth and the world. From everlasting to everlasting, Thou art God.

Oh Thou who art the giver of all good gifts, we thank Thee for this college that has been a home for truth, an inspirer of courage and faith to generations of women. For the vision and purpose of her who was its founder; for the long succession of those who in this place have dedicated heart and mind to the service of truth and freedom, we thank Thee. For her who has incarnated in dedicated leadership the living spirit of the founder, we thank Thee. And for those who have gone out from these halls to do heroic work in the world in fulfilment of ideals which have been their gift from this college, we thank Thee.

On this day of remembrance we pray Thee for the future of Mount Holyoke. Down through the vista of the years we may not look, but in faith we pray that she may go on from strength to strength making Thy way known upon earth.

And for this company assembled here from distant places to do reverence to the College, we pray Thee. Direct and govern all our thought. Make us mindful of our heritage in learning and in faith. Fill us with a due sense of the responsibility that we bear as daughters of Mount Holyoke. Unite us with all the company of brave spirits who have lived and worked and served Thee in this place, and lead us into the way of truth that we may hold the faith in unity of spirit and in the bond of peace. Amen.

MRS. WHITE: Our first speaker is an alumna, a graduate of the Class of 1920. She has been President of the Mount Holyoke Clubs at Cleveland and Chicago. She has served on the Board of Directors of the Chicago branch of the A.A.U.W. and on their Collegiate Bureau of Occupations. She represented Mount Holyoke on the Women's College Board for a Century of Progress, and is now its President. She has published many articles and traveled extensively. She is now Managing Editor of the *Journal of Land and Public Utility Economics*. Her keen mind and compelling personality are found in rare combination.

It gives me great pleasure to present to you, Miss Helen Monchow, who will speak to us on A Century of Mount Holyoke Scholarship. Dr. Monchow.

A CENTURY OF MOUNT HOLYOKE SCHOLARSHIP

HELEN CORBIN MONCHOW

*Managing Editor of The Journal of Land and
Public Utility Economics*

In meeting to celebrate this epoch in the history of Mount Holyoke we find ourselves in a unique position. Many institutions on a similar occasion have to look beyond their own doors to find the beginning and to pay tribute to the originator of the movement for which they stand. But we of Mount Holyoke do not have to look afield. We can claim as our own, on the one hand, the founder of higher education for women in America, who is at the same time the founder of our own Mount Holyoke. And as we span the century and look today at the fruits of Mary Lyon's pioneering and as we view the present high estate of women's education in this country, we find again within our own gates the woman who represents in her person and in her achievement the flowering of the first one hundred years of that movement. We can thus claim for our very own the epitome of the beginning of higher education for women in America and the epitome of its first one hundred years—Mary Lyon and Mary Emma Woolley.

Let us scan the interval—the one hundred years between these two great leaders. What are the contributions of Mount Holyoke to women's education in this period? What have these and other leaders within our ranks inspired the daughters of Mount Holyoke to accomplish?

The achievement of Mount Holyoke alumnae in scholarship was the topic assigned to me. We could spend considerable time in setting forth precisely what we mean by scholarship. But that is neither necessary nor desirable. We can all agree upon a broad definition of scholarship as pioneering in new fields of knowledge; the advancement of learning; the development of a discipline; a scientific method of approach. Not to all scholars is given the opportunity to add to the world's fund of knowledge, but all scholars by definition maintain and perpetuate the standards of high scholarship. The advancement of knowledge and the dissemination of knowledge are scarcely separable, especially when both functions are so frequently performed by the same individuals. What one generation contributes to the world's store of knowledge the next generation uses as a stepping stone to take off for new levels. The process is continuous. In both the creation of knowledge and in its spread Mount Holyoke has great traditions.

In the short space allotted it is not possible to be very specific—to list in detail the individuals who have made conspicuous contributions in scholarship. It is necessary therefore to name but a few—the ones who represent a group or a field, the types whose influence has been most clearly felt. In the process of such listing we can try to catch something of the flavor of the College and of the people who have made these one hundred years significant and so full of promise for the next century to come.

In attempting to cover these one hundred years in broad sweep it may help to divide them roughly into three periods. The division is not exact and no attempt is made to have it so. But we may consider first the fifty years from 1837 to 1887; then the period from the Semi-Centennial in 1887 to the turn of the century or thereabouts; and finally the years since 1900.

The first fifty years were a period when emphasis was laid on two things: first, the acquisition of knowledge as such and, second, its spread. These of necessity had to be the characteristics of that era. Opportunities for women to learn and to know had not been previously available. They had first to acquire the basic facts, the basic information before they could go on to explore, to discover new relationships, to create, to originate. Having learned themselves, they felt the responsibility to help others to know. They were imbued with the crusading spirit— the drive to extend to others the opportunities they themselves had enjoyed.

From the point of view of scholarship therefore these first years were characterized by emphasis on the acquisition of facts. The substance of the curriculum was meaty. A glance at the first catalogue is sufficient to prove the point. There we find among the textbooks used Olmsted's *Natural Philosophy*, Alexander's *Evidences of Christianity*, Wayland's *Moral Philosophy*, Marsh's *Ecclesiastical History*, and Smellie's *Philosophy of Natural History*. The instruction was marked by rigorous discipline. Thorough mastery through intensive study of a limited number of branches always with emphasis on the moral implications, a strong Christian influence, and inoculation with the spirit of evangelizing the world, educationally speaking—these were the heritage of Mount Holyoke alumnae in this first period.

What were the products of this heritage? Probably the most important was the sending out of a corps of able teachers, not only to carry on in established schools, but to pioneer in the founding of new schools and colleges. Schools for Negroes were established in the South, like the one which Sarah Dickey founded for Negro girls at Clinton, Mississippi. Schools for the Indians were started in the West. Maria Arms almost literally gave her life to teaching the Choctaw Indians; and Ellen Whitmore, Sarah Worcester, and Harriet Johnson were leading spirits in the Cherokee Female Seminary. Very small schools were often started in private homes which were frequently the first beginnings of educational opportunities in the frontier communities of this country. Thus we see Martha Newton, Oklahoma's first teacher, starting a school in Oklahoma City and maintaining it until the establishment of the public school system in that State. Finally, colleges of equal rank with Mount Holyoke were founded, some merely building on similar foundations, while others are direct offspring of our Alma Mater. These Daughter Colleges include Lake Erie College, Western College, Mills College, International Institute for Girls in Spain, and Huguenot College in South Africa. The seeds of a Mount Holyoke education were truly broadcast. The harvest was great.

The beginning of the second period, which has arbitrarily been set at 1887, marked more than a local transition, more than the change from seminary to college. This date coincides roughly at least with the flowering of the scientific spirit in this country, with the beginnings of graduate study for women, with the beginnings of specialization. In 1888 at the opening of the Marine Biological Laboratory at Woods Hole the very first assignment of a research project was made to our own Cornelia Clapp.

But the so-called scientific spirit was not new at Mount Holyoke. We had already had a long heritage in scientific study. It started with Mary Lyon. She, of course, has gone down in history for her contribution to women's education as an administrator, a pioneer advocate of establishing women's education on a permanent and firm foundation. But she must also be recognized for scholastic attainments, her aims and methods, and most particularly for her interest in and her stimulus to scientific research. In 1837, when women's education was in embryo, to have dared and to have persevered in including in the curriculum scientific studies along with the literary branches—these perhaps were the earmarks which have set off a Mount Holyoke education and Mount Holyoke scholastic standards and have given them the unique character which has colored their subsequent development.

Her example has been followed not only in the scientific field but in the arts and in the humanities as well. In the sciences we can follow the unbroken chain from teacher to pupil, pupil becoming teacher and so on down—from Mary Lyon to Lydia Shattuck, from Lydia Shattuck to Henrietta Hooker and Cornelia Clapp. The scientific approach, the evolutionary approach, and the laboratory method appeared early in the field of art as well. Beginning with the introduction of the course in The History of Art back in 1878—the first institution outside of Harvard to list such a course—followed by the introduction of the studio method, we can trace the succession of the teacher-pupil relation, with only a slight gap, from Elizabeth Blanchard to Louise Fitz-Randolph. In the humanities the line runs from Anna C. Edwards to Clara F. Stevens—two unusually long and significant careers. These will illustrate the lineage of Mount Holyoke scholarship. And the line of succession illustrates not only the student-teacher relation, but each of these leaders who has been cited also won for herself recognition in the field of scholarship; recognition beyond the limits of this campus; recognition for significant contributions to her particular field of learning. They have stimulated scholarly accomplishment and scholastic interest not only by their teaching but also by the example they have set.

It is not possible to trace the succession in all departments. Time does not permit. Besides, many of our present departments have only recently split off from the larger divisions; their own succession is not long; nevertheless it goes back to the history and evolution of the whole and shares the heritage of the whole.

What then of the last period—the years since the turn of the century? Its variety, largely as a result of specialization, defies detailed description. In general, the period may be characterized by emphasis on power over knowledge in contrast to acquisition of knowledge as such, the use of facts as opposed to the mere accumulation of facts.

Perhaps the simplest and most direct way to survey this era is to glance at the statistics concerning Mount Holyoke graduates in their scholastic activity since they left this campus. In the first place, more than 35 per cent of Mount Holyoke alumnae are now engaged in teaching or professional work—very positive evidence of an interest in scholastic achievement. But even more striking is the record concerning graduate study. Over 60 per cent of Mount Holyoke alumnae who replied to the questionnaire for the Biographical Directory have done some graduate study either in a college or university, in a professional school, or in special work. And of these last, about half have obtained graduate degrees and more than 10 per cent their doctorates. Truly this is a record to be proud of, especially when we stop to consider that graduate study for women is really a phenomenon of only the last fifty years. This record is evidence of a will to know, an interest in scholastic achievement, a response to the inspiration received at Mount Holyoke to go on to further pursuit of learning.

To round out the picture it is necessary to point out how much of this further study was made possible through recognition of work already done at Mount Holyoke. I refer to the record of our alumnae as recipients of scholarships, fellowships, grants-in-aid from other colleges and universities, from foundations, from research organizations, and the like. Each year as the awards are made by these various organizations, the list of Mount Holyoke graduates included therein is impressive evidence of the recognition of the standards of scholarship maintained at Mount Holyoke.

The individual accomplishments of the period are reflected in the long list of Mount Holyoke writers, teachers, librarians, doctors, educational administrators, curators, editors, archaeologists, psychiatrists, poets, nurses, and a whole galaxy of research workers in special fields too numerous to mention.

What is the essence of Mount Holyoke's contribution to scholarship? It also, like so many of our traditions, ideals, and achievements, is probably traceable to Mary Lyon, to her emphasis on social usefulness as the true purpose of education. The application of the term has broadened. When Mary Lyon used it, it applied largely to social usefulness in the field of teaching, either here or in the foreign field. Today social usefulness has a much broader significance—broader as the opportunities for women are broader, again largely as a result of Mary Lyon's efforts. But I think the same spirit prevails today. We have a tradition for doing things worth while. There is work in the world to do and Mount Holyoke alumnae have always been in the forefront of the doers.

We have done this work thoroughly, competently, working from the sound foundations which we were taught to recognize and to appreciate in our undergraduate days at Mount Holyoke. Here our heritage of long emphasis on the scientific method has stood us in good stead. Our interest in the causes of things, in the institutions which are the media through which social change takes place, in the underlying forces that motivate human activity, these are the products of our scientific background.

And always Mount Holyoke scholastic endeavor has been characterized by vigor, ruggedness, a pioneering spirit, and above all, enthusiasm and imagination. The pictures that have come down to us of Mary Lyon show her to have been a person of great physical energy, attacking each new problem with all her tremendous stock of vitality and enthusiasm. We see her successors scouring the surrounding countryside gathering specimens to fill up Williston Hall, unearthing treasures of scientific value. All this was done in the spirit of eagerness to know and with the thrill of exploration. A story told about Lydia Shattuck will illustrate these qualities. It was after she had retired. One day in the spring a caller found her looking out the window at the budding trees. She looked very happy, as if pleased with her thoughts. When asked what made her so, she replied that she was thinking of "all the little laboratories in all the little leaves on all the trees."

During the course of one hundred years we have celebrated four anniversaries. The first in 1862, after twenty-five years, was devoted to reminiscences of Mary Lyon, tributes to her character and to her accomplishments, a "festival of remembrance" as one speaker on that occasion called it. The second in 1887, after fifty years, coincided with a turning point, the transition from seminary to college. Incidentally that celebration also took place in a pouring rain. One onlooker commented: "Thursday morning's procession, hidden under umbrellas and waterproofs, was watched from the Seminary windows by many whom pru-

dence forbade to encounter the storm." The third anniversary
in 1912, after seventy-five years, was a jubilee. The College had
blossomed after the disaster of 1896, its campus had begun to
take on the appearance we see today, the curriculum and the
college status were established and promised long and continuous service in advancing women's education. Now, after another twenty-five years, we meet to celebrate another and
greater epoch. We can pay tribute to the achievements of
the last quarter century and we do so with pride and affection. But we may also look back over the whole one hundred
years of our College and try to fit this anniversary into its setting in relation both to the past and to the future.

In this day of transition and rapidly shifting scenes, perhaps
we would do best to vow to keep alive the enthusiasm for know-
ing and for doing, the ruggedness, the vigor, and the pioneering
spirit. There is need for them all. Mount Holyoke alumnae have
helped to push out the frontiers of education; they have helped
to push out the frontiers of knowledge; it still remains for them
to help push out the frontiers of opportunity for women, to help
women—not because they are women but because of their actual and potential contribution to society—to win the recognition, the rewards, and the increased opportunities for which
their education and scholastic achievements have and are fitting them.

MRS. WHITE: We are all proud of our next speaker, also an
alumna of Mount Holyoke College, and the first woman to be
a member of the Cabinet of the President of the United States.
She has held many positions in the interest of social service and
public welfare. In 1933 she was awarded the medal for eminent
achievement by the American Women's Association. I am honored to introduce to you the Secretary of Labor of the United
States, Miss Frances Perkins, who will speak to us on The Rôle
of the College Woman in the Community. Miss Perkins.

THE RÔLE OF THE COLLEGE WOMAN IN THE COMMUNITY

Frances Perkins

Secretary of Labor

As we have listened to the paper which has just been read, I think most of us have come again to the realization that the strength of the past is the inspiration of the future, and I noted by your ready response to what the speaker had to say the indication that each of us was thinking ahead, wishfully, that there might be many more coming forth from this college in the years to come who could carry the torch which she so well described, the torch of scholarship and character and faith.

And as one thinks, too, about what this college has meant in the community in which it has served, the larger community of the United States, one realizes that certain deep spiritual and moral values have always been at the back of the strength which its faculty showed, which its endowments developed, which its graduates illustrated. A certain faith in the possibilities of life upon this planet certainly has motivated all that has been done here, a definite acceptance, an enthusiasm for the conception that each human soul has great worth and dignity, a strength of belief and an enthusiasm for the idea that it is possible for the human race by taking thought infinitely to improve itself.

And upon this program, many generations have gone out from this college, determined to make that part of the world with which they had contact a somewhat more favorable place for the development and the improvement of the human race, and with a complete faith in those possibilities.

You will tell me that these are, after all, but the basic principles of the Christian religion, and that is true. But so is the conception of generalized education a part of that basic principle of the understanding and belief in the worth and dignity of individuals and their capacity to improve themselves and the human race. So we are, after all, in this institution, but one of the agencies for the gradual improvement of the world and the race.

And how has this been done in the past? As the last paper indicated, it has been done largely by the development of disciplines, disciplines which the human race was able to accept and to impose upon itself—the discipline of order, the discipline of sincerity, the discipline of character, the discipline of behavior, the discipline of responsibility.

These are great achievements, and people who can for themselves win the battle of self-discipline have always made a contribution to the community in which they live, and in so far as the women who have accepted education here from the hands of disciplined people, in so far as they have accepted it and the discipline that goes with education, they are making and building up the one thing which this world today needs more than anything else, the discipline of reason, the discipline that makes it possible for an educated man or woman to maintain a calm view of even disturbed and disordered behaviors, to look for truth, to believe in truth, and to practice those habits of life which make it possible to know truth and select from that knowledge the general trends which are leading upward, discarding trends of behavior which are leading to destruction.

More and more educated and disciplined men and women are approaching the realization that the progress which must still be made by the human race in this world, cannot be a progress of force; it must be as Plato said in the *Timaeus* so many years ago, "Creation is the victory of persuasion, not the victory of force." And with that kind of motto the self-discipline and the part played by the habit of discipline must go forward, not only in this country, but in the world.

I want to express a sense of thanksgiving for just a moment here this morning that there has been so much of the spirit of calm, of discipline, of wisdom and judgment in the continuing leadership of this college. It has been impressed upon those who have gone out from this college. This leadership has been a blessed thing, and one for which Mount Holyoke women are continually grateful to you, Miss Woolley.

An airplane view of this country reveals that it is made up, like a huge patchwork quilt, of many communities differing greatly in character. But because all these sections are found together within the confines of the United States of America they may be considered to constitute one big national community with an almost bewildering variety of interests. There are large and small cities, towns and rural areas. There are centers illustrative of our civilization in its most advanced stages in contrast with sections exceedingly backward in the march of progress. Each type of community has its advantages and disadvantages, its needs and problems. Each has its own people trying to live their own lives, to get as much out of their existence as they can; and connected with almost every community are some people at least who are trying to give as much as possible of their services to help others. Thus in each community is being enacted constantly the pulsating drama of living, participated in by many different types of people with different experiences, different desires and objectives. We shall not attempt to enumerate all these types, but just to throw the spotlight on one—the college woman.

There are not far from a million women college graduates living in this country today, according to a recent estimate by the United States Office of Education. These women are scattered around, thickly in some spots and sparsely in others. What rôles are they taking in the scenes of their immediate surroundings and what is their part in the bit of national drama that includes and transcends all local activities?

It is impossible to give more than a fragmentary answer to this question for lack of time and comprehensive data. Under the circumstances we might select an average and more or less composite community as did Robert and Helen Lynd in their survey of current community problems entitled *Middletown*, and thus we might analyze the relationship of the local college women, educated at various institutions throughout the land, to the varied activities of such a representative center. Or another way of painting the picture of the college woman's share in our broad community life—and the one which we plan to employ this morning—is to take all the living graduates from one particular college and trace them along their diverging lines from the halls of their common Alma Mater to the many varied settings wherein they are spinning the threads of their individual existences and at the same time are weaving definite patterns in the fabric of community life.

The means for such an analysis lie at hand. We have valuable information of particular interest to us, in a report just completed under the direction of Ruth Olmsted Truex of our own Department of Economics and Sociology and entitled Mount Holyoke Alumnae Centennial Census. This study was made with the idea of compiling data on all the living alumnae—graduates and non-graduates—of Mount Holyoke, but the report in question analyzes only the status and achievements of something over five thousand graduates who answered the questionnaire sent to all women who had ever attended Mount Holyoke.

The study might appear to be of double significance to us— giving the present picture of the graduates of our own Alma Mater and a cross section of the adaptation of college women to life in a constantly changing world. And concerning the relationship of such changes to the college woman's rôle and destiny I shall have more to say presently.

First, let us see what has happened to the graduates who have left this delightful stage of academic training for the more challenging activities in the broader arena of the world.

In considering the activities of college women, we may divide them into two big classes: those who are engaged, according to the Census phraseology, in gainful occupation, that is, those who receive for their services a definite remuneration, a wage, salary, commission, or fee; and those who receive no set monetary reward for their contributions to society. The report on our graduates shows that of the approximately five thousand graduates who gave information as to their occupational status, slightly over a half were gainfully occupied, 42 per cent reported that they were engaged in home making, not quite 2 per cent had retired from active work, and slightly more than 2 per cent stated that they had no occupation.

Let us consider first the home-making group, who would consist largely of the married women. It is of interest to see what proportion of the graduates are married, in view of the question constantly being asked as to what extent college women follow the normal traditions of women in regard to matrimony. The figures show that 51.9 per cent of the Mount Holyoke living graduates have married, as compared with 73.5 per cent of the total female population 15 years of age and over reported as having been married, according to the 1930 Census. This seems to explode the fear that college women are too high-browed or too preoccupied with other pursuits to want to marry or to be wanted in marriage. Among the married graduates of Mount Holyoke the divorcees constituted only a very small percentage, a little over 1 per cent. Thus there seems to be a fifty-fifty chance that the college woman will have a normal married life in a community. She is much more apt, than not, to marry a college man, if the Mount Holyoke study is typical, as three-fourths of the graduates had husbands who were also college graduates.

It is of interest to analyze briefly the type of work of the husbands since this is more or less indicative of the kind of community where the married women graduates are living and suggestive of the part they may be playing in such environment. They are not living on farms, to any extent, since less than 4 per cent reported husbands in agricultural work. On the other hand, somewhat over half of the husbands were professional men, including notably substantial proportions who were engaged in teaching, engineering, and religious work, and as lawyers and physicians. Over a third were business men, of whom about half were executives, proprietors, or managers.

Though the vast majority of women with professional and business husbands would be living in cities and towns, and putting down rather deep roots into a particular community, other women, particularly those married to clergymen or engineers might find themselves leading a somewhat roving existence and oftentimes going to the outposts of civilization to share with their husbands something of the pioneers' rôle.

The husband's vocation is also quite often an influential factor in prescribing many of the activities in which his college wife is expected to engage. The wife, for example, of a big business executive, a minister, a college professor, or even a doctor or lawyer, has usually a rather definitely channeled course to follow in community affairs. The college woman, in many instances, because of her intelligent way of sharing her husband's responsibilities, deserves considerable credit for his success.

The matter of family income is also highly influential in shaping the rôle of the college woman, determining whether she has to devote herself almost exclusively to being a home maker; whether she is forced by economic need to add a wage-earning career to her home-making job, with very little time and energy available for other community interests; or whether she has sufficient paid help in the home to give her considerable leisure for participation in affairs outside the home. The married graduates of Mount Holyoke fall largely into the middle-income class. It must be remembered that the family income reported included a wife's earnings and income as well as the husband's.

I think that all persons concerned with the question of future citizenship are interested in the number of children which college women have since they would seem to be well-qualified for motherhood, socially, intellectually, and physically on the whole, and financially in most instances. Two-thirds of the married women had children, the average number of children being 1.6. Some of the earlier classes had a few families with eight or more children, while for the graduates of more recent years—disregarding for such comparison the most recent classes, or those from 1927 on—we find rarely more than four children in a family.

As the statistics presented in the report do not show how many of the married women were also in gainful occupation we shall not attempt to go into this question, but shall present simply a bird's-eye view of occupational trends among all the graduates, irrespective of marital status.

As we have already seen, over two-fifths reported home making as their job in life, this constituting the largest of the various occupational groups. The next largest group or one-fifth of those stating their occupations, were teachers, and of these approximately a half were teaching in secondary schools, and about a fourth in colleges. The rôle of the teacher in a community is acknowledged to be of paramount importance since she shares more or less with the parents the opportunity to mold boys and girls in the formative periods of their lives. Thus college women have always rendered and are still rendering valuable service in the capacity of teachers, although the data in the Mount Holyoke report indicate that whereas there was a rather consistent increase in the proportions of teachers up through the Class of 1911, in later classes there has been some fluctuation with a dropping off for three of the four class groups arranged in five-year periods. This is probably due to the fact that women have had opening up to them new kinds of occupational opportunities, particularly in other professions. In general the data for the Mount Holyoke alumnae show substantial numbers as librarians and social workers. In both of these rôles college women have been making valuable contributions, gradually increasing in importance as the need for such services in communities has become recognized as highly essential for a welfare program.

Especially in the comparatively new field of social service col
lege women are today playing an exceedingly varied and valuable part, both in repairing bad rents and strengthening weak
spots in our whole social fabric and in helping to develop
stronger and more durable texture in the form of better,
healthier, more reliable citizens to meet the social and economic wear and tear of our present complicated civilization.
Private employment in social work has been for some years and
continues to be a form of employment for a conspicuous number of our college women as many different types of service have
developed. A much more recent development in this field, which
I shall merely mention here and refer to later is public welfare work sponsored by the local and national Government.

Among the Mount Holyoke graduates are goodly sprinklings
of women in research and scientific work. There are 69 alumnae
who are authors, 31 are physicians, and 7 are lawyers. Then
there are 49 in the religious field, as Young Women's Christian
Association workers, missionaries, and so on. There is a total
of 186 in the field of business including proprietors, executives,
managers, saleswomen, advertisers, statisticians. Not far from
400 reported themselves to be in secretarial and clerical work,
155 of whom had graduated since 1931. No doubt necessity
rather than choice is largely responsible for this situation. Probably the depression and restricted opportunities in other vocational avenues have forced a number of the recent graduates to
accept secretarial and clerical rôles. Some have perhaps taken
such jobs because of the growing importance attached to the
services of a good secretary while others may have taken such
employment as a stepping stone to another and more desired
vocation.

With broad sweeps of the brush we have merely outlined the
chief occupations of the Mount Holyoke alumnae as representative college graduates, but many more detailed strokes would be
necessary to give a true representation of the value of the rôles
they are enacting. But there is also another side to the picture

which calls for attention, an aspect presented in the report by only a few bare statistics, showing that nearly half of the alumnae reporting were actively participating in social and civic vol unteer organizations, while approximately a third reported similar interests in educational and religious activities.

Behind such statistics, we realize, lies a great volume of interesting and valuable contributions by college women to their particular communities and to the nation as a whole. I think that we may truly say that women's organizations in this country are a tremendous force for progress. Through such means women are one of the great present factors in developing public opinion for meeting changing conditions and therefore they are playing a part of primary importance in national and international affairs. They are achieving this end even though the actual number who occupy important public positions is exceedingly small.

Thus it is of interest to consider briefly how varied women's organizations are in nature, how much they have in common, and what part college women are taking in promoting and carrying out their programs. These organizations are so numerous that it would be impossible to try even to call the roll of all. Each one is concerned primarily with objectives in a particular field. For example, some are concerned with educational matters as related to women such as the college clubs and the American Association of University Women; some handle educational problems in general or as related to children. Then there are the many associations of women built up on a foundation of general professional and business interests or on a particular vocational basis, such as law, medicine, nursing, art, writing, home economics and so on. A number are basically religious and tied up with a special creed or sect, while some are concerned with character building. Others are definitely cultural or scientific. Quite a few deal with matters of social welfare, or with economic, industrial, or labor problems. Some have as their chief objectives better citizenship or better legislation, or better health. Some are working for the prevention of war and maintenance of peace. Some are concerned with community projects and consumers' interests and others are fraternal, patriotic, or political.

Despite their diversity of interests the great majority of these organizations have some similar planks in their platforms. Thus they have a common meeting ground and can be rallied to support efforts to reach certain worth while local and national objectives, such as the promotion of health, peace, and women and child welfare, social security measures, higher educational standards, political reform, better legislation, better citizenship, cultural standards and development, to mention the most outstanding aims. Most of these organizations are nation-wide in their set-up, ready to be galvanized into activity for a particular cause by a dynamic appeal from the national headquarters.

It is difficult to say exactly to what extent college women are responsible for these organizations and their achievements except that their membership includes thousands of women who have had the benefits of a college education, that in many of the organizations college women predominate and play the rôle of leaders, and that many college women belong to a number of different organizations. Recently, I was interested to see, in a list of Mount Holyoke alumnae being considered as candidates for an alumna trustee for our Alma Mater, the varied organizations with which each was affiliated. For example, I pick one of those recommended candidates at random. I find that she is the wife of a banker, and has one son, that she has been a teacher and speaker in this and foreign countries; that she is now a trustee of a particular school and member of its board in her city; chairman formerly of the International Institute of the local Young Women's Christian Association; vice-president of a local women's club; member of the board of directors of the Leisure Time Activities, Inc., of her city; a member of the League of Women Voters, the Art Club, Foreign Policy Association, Appalachian Mountain Club, and Agawam Hunt Club.

She is a lecturer on current events and "is considered in the community as a woman of outstanding ability." I believe that such a description may be taken as more or less characteristic of hundreds of our college women today.

This alumna illustrates not only so many of the trends which we have been discussing but others besides. Her interest in art, sports, and current events are rather typical, it would seem, since the report on the Mount Holyoke graduates shows that over half were devoting part of their leisure time to intellectual activities, over two-fifths reported an active interest in some kind of sports, and a fourth were giving some time to art.

In still another way the alumna's activities just described represent a rôle many college women are called in to perform, namely to serve, without remuneration but because of a public-spirited attitude, on public welfare or school boards or those connected with philanthropic agencies, or institutions. Such services rendered by able and well-trained women without any idea of personal gain and advancement are of incalculable value in many communities.

In the changing times in which we are living there is an increasing demand and opportunity for college women to take part in public affairs, both as volunteers and on a remunerative basis. It is a generally recognized fact that women on the whole have a strong social and humanitarian viewpoint; and if they have given special study to such problems as have many college women, they excel rather strikingly in various kinds of public service, in which even when they are paid for their work the factor of monetary profits is not the objective.

The Mount Holyoke report does not indicate to what extent its alumnae are going into this field, but we do know that in the past fifteen years, partly because woman suffrage has opened up some public offices to women and partly because of the development of the social sciences and the increasing importance given them in the curriculum of women's colleges, there has been a steadily growing infiltration of women into county, city, state,

and federal government service. For example we see a few college women seeking public office through election to a state leg-
islature and possibly an occasional college woman aspiring to a
seat in the United States Congress, not because they want to
engage in the game of politics, but because they have a zest for
the science of politics and good government. There is need for
well-trained and capable women to take part in the enactment
of state and federal laws, helping in this way to write into such
legislation the best feminine viewpoint, which is essential for a
well-balanced government. We see just a handful of college
women receiving appointments to the state and federal government jobs. Not political influence but ability to do the job
has got these places for women. They have qualified because
of ability. There should be more women in such positions. Why
shouldn't public service be the field for many college-graduated
women who do not have to earn a living but who wish to be
useful to their communities? Why shouldn't they demand political recognition, not for personal advantage, but for the opportunity to serve?

But a much more striking trend is the substantial number of
college women entering through the medium of civil service or
a merit system into many kinds of jobs, in the state departments of labor, health, or public welfare. Also, there has been
a conspicuous increase in the numbers of college women in the
federal government service in the past twenty years. Personnel
records in the various agencies at Washington show many college women doing outstanding and interesting work as statisticians, research experts, and scientists in an astounding variety
of lines, as social workers, lawyers, doctors, nurses, writers, editors, educators, teachers, historians, librarians, dietitians, art-
ists, to mention only the most conspicuous. Such facts are
convincing proof that women can pursue their chosen voca-
tions in the realm of public service. If time permitted such
detailed information could be given showing how many college
women, whose names are not generally known to the public,

are playing a truly vital rôle in our national life, making valuable contributions to our store of knowledge, helping to shape policies and to chart programs and procedures.

The past few years appear to many of us to have inevitably hastened the development of a new order which seems to be opening up new opportunities particularly for well-trained and public-spirited women to fit into new kinds of activities. Certainly a challenge comes to all college women today to get a true understanding of the changes in our social order, the reasons for these changes, and the ways in which to adapt themselves to such developments.

To help with the understanding of the somewhat modified rôle that many college women are being asked to enact today, I would like in conclusion to sketch briefly certain trends of the past few years. As we look back to the depths of the depression we realize that our whole national civilization was threatened with collapse, because of so many operations thrown completely out of balance and widespread breakdowns in regard to other activities. Loss of employment, loss of income, loss of home, toboggan slides in wages and salaries, destitution and suffering in many directions made it imperative for the federal and state governments to step into the breach in a great many ways, as never before in our history.

Thus from its very beginning the New Deal had to formulate rapidly an emergency program to combat the depression on all fronts. This meant almost overnight creation and development of a number of new agencies, such as those extending special aid to crippled business and financial interests, to hard-pressed farmers and home owners, to the unemployed, the victims of depressed labor standards, the destitute, and so on. Thus we have seen in a few short years tremendous new enterprises started by the Federal Government working in conjunction with state governments charged with the responsibility of carrying on a nation-wide economic, social and humanitarian program hitherto not tried and hardly conceived in our country.

We have seen, for example, both a public works and a works relief program as well as emergency relief measures inaugurated, each of which will probably be combined to be handled in some form and to some extent as a permanent part of governmental responsibility as was not the case prior to the depression.

We have seen launched a much-needed and long-delayed social security program on a vast and varied scale with a federal-state set-up which promises progress in regard to social selfare in general and special aid to children, women, and handicapped groups in our population. We have seen the Federal Government now being definitely aided by state legislatures, trying to formulate a better labor program and thereby to promote the general welfare of wage earners, by shortening hours of work, increasing wages and purchasing power of millions of people, by insuring workers the principle of collective bargaining and by guaranteeing the opportunity for employment. All these measures have been inaugurated by specific pieces of legislation. We have seen the effort to restore and improve our whole economic set-up to protect the savings and investments of the people, to strengthen our national relations by building up sounder financial foundations and operations, and to forward our international relations through trade agreements and peace programs.

We have witnessed special attention given by our central government as never before to people's homes, to the complicated and urgent problems of mortgages on homes, to slum clearance, and proposals for better housing for large groups of our people. We have watched the launching of big projects of tremendous and social significance, far-reaching in area and effect, to bring progress to our rural and small-town areas, to our backward or depleted regions.

Not only have various new agencies been created to carry out these programs, but these programs are tied in at many points with the functions of the old-line agencies, thus increasing and amplifying their work in many ways, and calling for closer cooperation between the Federal and State Government.

MARY E. WOOLLEY
President 1900–1937

I have given this brief recital for two reasons. First, because all of these new trends may possibly influence in some way your occupational rôle; and secondly, because they are of interest to you in your rôle of citizens, demanding your attention, your understanding and your support, in those ways which will make the United States of America the best possible form of democracy.

And here as a suitable finish to this discussion I should like to give John Dewey's definition of progress as one "of discovering the needs and capacities of collective human nature, and of inventing the social machinery which will set available powers operating for the satisfaction of those needs." This is indeed a challenging rôle—the rôle of being a true progressive in our great national community life, a rôle all college women are asked to assume.

MRS. WHITE: For thirty-seven years Mount Holyoke has been, we might say, President Woolley. A graduate of Brown University, a former Professor of Wellesley College, the recipient of more honorary degrees than we can enumerate, ranking among this country's foremost administrators, one of the world's most sincere peace advocates, the only woman delegate to the Disarmament Conference at Geneva in 1932. I present President Mary E. Woolley, who will speak to you on Mount Holyoke in the International Field. President Woolley.

MOUNT HOLYOKE IN THE INTERNATIONAL FIELD

MARY E. WOOLLEY

"Among the budding apple trees of a hilltop campus," begins a recent story of Mount Holyoke's Centennial. From that hilltop campus for one hundred years have gone daughters to all parts of the United States, into home and school, scientific laboratory and business office, into service of church and state.

If the limits of Mount Holyoke's work were those of the nation, we might well be proud of what the Seminary and College have accomplished within these years. One of the most amazing aspects of the life of your Alma Mater, however, is the fact that it has *not* been limited to this country, that even one hundred years ago there was a world vision. One hundred years ago! Think of what that implies. Isolation; distance and difficulty and danger; almost insuperable barriers between hemisphere and hemisphere. It is only as we put ourselves back into the social and political life of the first half of the nineteenth century that we can appreciate what "world vision" meant in the eighteen-forties.

Mount Holyoke women who have gone out as missionaries since the opening of the Seminary in 1837 number 386, according to the records; eighty-seven to China; forty-seven to Japan; seventy-two to India; sixty to Turkey; twenty-six to Africa; eight to Persia; eighty-six to other countries, such as Hawaii, formerly a foreign land; Mexico, and among Indian tribes in the unsettled West, infinitely farther from New England in those days than any part of the world today.

But that tells less of the story than figures usually reveal. The numbers given do not include those who have taught in foreign Daughter Colleges and other foreign schools after they had graduated from mission board support. The essential is not numbers of alumnae, or the regions to which they went. The task which they accomplished is the significant part of the record. That record is a history in itself; all that I can hope to do within the few moments that are mine is to direct your thought along three lines of accomplishment: educational, social, political.

These missionaries were first of all educators. Like a drama is the story of education carried throughout the world by daughters of Mount Holyoke from the day in Persia when a leading Nestorian Bishop led two little girls, seven and ten years of age, to Fidelia Fiske, and putting their hands in hers, said

"They are your daughters; no man shall take them from your hand," adding: "Now you begin Mount Holyoke in Persia." All along the line from Fidelia Fiske to this very day that we celebrate, Mount Holyoke women have been demonstrating the truth of Deacon Safford's comment concerning the re-carpeting of Seminary Hall: "The times demand it. The education of the world is being carried on here." In every country to which the alumnae went, they were founders and builders of schools. No channel of Mount Holyoke's influence has been wider, deeper or more constant than this of education. What she has done in this country is thrilling; what she has accomplished in other lands is even more dramatic.

During six months spent in China several years ago, visiting many communities in Northern, Central and Southeastern China, there was only one where I failed to find Mount Holyoke teachers, and that was my own fault, in arriving just after a Mount Holyoke alumna had left! I hardly need add that at the two outstanding colleges for women in that country, Ginling at Nanking and the College for Women affiliated with Yenching University in Peking, Mount Holyoke women were at the head, Matilda Calder Thurston, President of Ginling; Alice Browne Frame, Dean of Women at Yenching.

If we turn to Japan, Kobe College has on its staff Mount Holyoke graduates who have stood by for many a year, and Matsuyama High School has a special claim upon our interest because of the "humble and human and merry-hearted and live-with-able person," Olive Hoyt,—so described by her associates —who is its presiding genius, to list only two of many institutions.

China and Japan might be taken as symbols of the part Seminary and College have played in education the world around. It has been said that the influence of the educational activity of the missionaries "was in many lands as permanent and concrete as anything wrought by schools in America." Persia, Turkey, China, Japan, India and Ceylon, Africa and

Spain, Hawaii and Mexico all played a part. And the types were as varied as the regions in which they appeared. From kindergarten to university, there is literally no stage of education not represented. Fidelia Fiske's "Little Holyoke" in Urumia; Charlotte and Mary Ely's "Mount Holyoke Seminary of Kurdistan, 'deep in the mountains of Turkey'";—I hardly dare mention names in the Near East because of the impossibility of including all. No part of the world is more indebted to Mount Holyoke than just this section.

It is interesting that today in "nationalized Turkey" the influence of the old schools, some closed, some destroyed, still goes on, many of the teachers in the new national schools having been trained in the ones founded by Mount Holyoke women.

I cannot turn from the Near East without a thought of one of those valiant teachers who for forty years gave her life to Marash, more than two-thirds of the time as Principal of the Central Turkey Girls College. The work in Turkey is made more vivid to us because the last years of her life, ending so unexpectedly a few months ago, Ellen Blakely spent here.

I said "Like a drama is the story of education carried throughout the world by daughters of Mount Holyoke." True in every land, in none is it more true than in India, Burma and Ceylon. Again I hesitate to mention names "for the time would fail me to tell" of Ballantines, Fairbankses, Hardings, Howlands, Humes, Scudders, who, interwoven with the century of progress in that land, are also a part of Mount Holyoke's history. Alice Van Doren of 1903, Educational Secretary of the National Christian Council of India, Burma and Ceylon, within the last few weeks, writes that even to outline the story of Mount Holyoke's connections with those countries would involve an amount of research far beyond her resources. And, the end is not yet! Do you know that today nineteen Mount Holyoke women are living within the Indian Empire? Of these nineteen, by far the largest group is connected with the Women's Christian College, Madras, the Oriental sister college to Mount Holyoke. Founded in 1914, for twenty-two years this college has been to South India what Mount Holyoke was to New England during the early days, a pioneer of education and progress among women just emerging into a new era.

The Principal of this "sister college" of ours is an English woman, Eleanor McDougall, formerly Lecturer in Classics at Westfield College, London, our daughter by adoption, for we honored ourselves by conferring upon her an honorary degree several years ago. The Vice-Principal, Edith Coon, is a "regular daughter" as well as by the distinction of an honorary degree. Always there are Mount Holyoke women on the staff. This year, for the second time, Professor Stokey of our Department of Botany is on leave to substitute at Madras, and Mary E. Wells, one of our alumnae and Professor of Mathematics at Vassar, has been there for a semester. Truly "anyone with imagination can easily realize something of what has been done to put science and mathematics 'on the map' among South Indian students at a time when scientific knowledge and the scientific habit of mind are essential to the rapid developments taking place in Indian life and thought."

Mount Holyoke is proud of her five Daughter Colleges. It is significant that two of the five are in another hemisphere, the International Institute at Madrid and Huguenot College in South Africa. I wonder whether anyone who knew Alice Gordon Gulick can give an impersonal appraisal of her and her work for the women of Spain. My first impression I received when she came to speak at my father's church during my own college days; my last when she visited her Alma Mater after I began my work here. And always in her presence it seemed to me that I was in the presence of royalty! A woman of rare charm of personality, of rare strength of character, no college could have had an ambassador of good will more truly representative of nobility, the nobility of the human race.

In these days of tragedy for Spain, one's thoughts turn often to the beautiful buildings of the International Institute in

Madrid, to the Spanish women who by their scholarship and character have won not only honor for themselves, for their country and for the mother college, but also opportunity for their countrywomen. Today their college is a place of refuge in the unspeakable horrors of civil war. Tomorrow, we believe it will be again a leader in the Spain of a happier future.

It was my good fortune to know also the first Principal and President of Mount Holyoke's daughter in South Africa, Abbie Ferguson and her co-worker and successor, Anna Bliss. I should like to have known Dr. Andrew Murray, whose desire for a school in South Africa "on the plan of that in South Hadley" meant the beginning of Huguenot Seminary and College. I love his letter in answer to one from Mount Holyoke, saying that both Miss Ferguson and Miss Bliss were ready for the new work so far away; "We asked for one teacher and the Lord has given us two, accompanying His answer with passage money for both, without delay."

Today Huguenot College is an integral part of the University of South Africa. "It is doubtful" wrote the *Cape Times* Editor of President Ferguson, "whether any woman, certainly no woman from outside, has ever made so deep an impression upon the life of South Africa."

"The missionary movement overran the world with dogged idealism," to quote from *Seminary Militant*. That idealism expressed itself in social service, in a multitude of ways, chief among them medical service. Ellen Bartholomew Scudder, spending thirty-five years in medical work in India, and, incidentally, bringing up three sons and two daughters; Ida Scudder of 1925, just finishing five years at Vellore, training young Indian women "to carry the medical skill of the West into hospitals, towns and villages," are typical of Mount Holyoke's internationalism along the line of social work.

Also significant is the social work carried on in India today by Indian graduates of the College, Dora Maya Das, Edith D'Lima and Vimala Appasamy, and in Ceylon by Grace Paul.

Mount Holyoke has played a part in the international field along political lines, using that word in its original and truer meaning. Alice Gordon Gulick in the late nineties, working among the 1600 Spanish prisoners of war on Seavey's Island off the coast of New Hampshire from Portsmouth; Annie Allen, unofficial representative of American interests with the Turkish government, of whom Admiral Bristol, then American High Commissioner at Constantinople cabled: "I cannot pay too high tribute to noble character Allen. During three years I have marveled at courage endurance she showed in traveling all over Anatolia in all seasons year in service humanity. She was known throughout country from highest official to lowest peasant. She traveled without fear because unknowing what fear was"; and a host of Mount Holyoke alumnae, conspicuous and inconspicuous, have helped to further world understanding.

For a century Mount Holyoke has gone out to the daughters of the world; for the last quarter century the world has sent its daughters to Mount Holyoke. There were representatives of other nations and races at Seminary and College before the Great War, but it is only since that period that the College has become truly cosmopolitan in its student body. China, Japan, Korea, India, Ceylon, Turkey, Armenia, Yugoslavia, Czechoslovakia, Greece, Italy, Switzerland, France, Germany, U.S.S.R., Bulgaria, Hungary, Venezuela, Chile, Uruguay—we have had representatives of them all as undergraduates or graduate students. I have omitted our first cousins, English, Canadian, Scotch, whom we have welcomed, for they hardly seem to belong within the designation of "foreign."

That "international is a word with which to conjure among the students at Mount Holyoke" has been said more than once. Is it strange? "Internationalism" has been woven into the very warp and woof of this institution from the beginning.

Mary Lyon had a vision—Frances Perkins reminded us of that on Founder's Day a few years ago—a world-wide vision. It was not couched in the twentieth century vernacular. It interpreted "salvation" in terms of the individual rather than of the world-wide family, but its understanding of what is essential to the realization of internationalism is singularly akin to that which the world is approaching, albeit by painful steps and slow. I learned a great deal during my six months in Geneva, at the Conference for the Reduction and Limitation of Armaments, and chief among the lessons was the conviction that the salvation of the world would not be brought about by formulae! "It is not the Covenant of the League but humanity that needs to be reformed," said Rumania's minister for Foreign Affairs.

A year or two ago, I found, not in a sermon, but in *Harper's Magazine*, these words: "It is not technical knowledge that is going to save us, it is increased proficiency in the great province of human relations. If being good can save us, it is high time we tried it. Education in the ordinary sense won't save us. We want something that works faster; something, if possible, that changes men. Every steeple that points to the sky has a message, to wit: that our visible world is geared to a world invisible from which it can derive power and even wisdom for the regulation of human life."

On all sides among thinking men and women, there is a growing conviction that the future of the world depends not only upon the cultivation of the "things of the mind" but also upon the cultivation of the "things of the spirit." And we turn back to Mary Lyon with a more understanding appreciation of her vision a century ago.

AWARDS OF THE ALUMNAE MEDAL OF HONOR

MRS. WHITE: It has seemed fitting at this time when Mount Holyoke College is celebrating its Centennial for the Alumnae Association to express its deep appreciation for the distinguished services rendered by alumnae to the College. Hundreds of names have come to mind of graduates who by their work in their special fields, in their communities and homes, are honoring their Alma Mater. The Committee of which Mrs. Louis W. Arnold, of Waban, Massachusetts, is Chairman, has chosen a few names typical of those we wish to honor under the following definition formulated by the Committee. "The medal is awarded by the Mount Holyoke Alumnae Association for eminent service in promoting the effectiveness of the Alumnae Association, for signal service in completing definite projects undertaken by the College, or for other noteworthy services which strengthen the position of the College."

I have the pleasure to present at this time for the Alumnae Medals of Honor the following alumnae. The citations will be read by President Woolley.

Lucy Cope Shelmire, Class of 1877; who for sixty years has served her College in every important way, as President of the Alumnae Association, during whose régime the Alumnae Council was formed, as a member of the Board of Trustees, as Honorary President of the Philadelphia Club; bringing to each of these offices wide experience and wisdom, as well as the more intangible influence of a gracious spirit, thus in every relationship reflecting honor on her Alma Mater.

Mary Dudley Willcox, Class of 1878; loyally serving the College as member of the Board of Trustees; as Chairman of the Building Committee throughout eight years; to whose understanding of ways and means, of beauty and use, the Student-Alumnae Hall bears eloquent tribute, proving day by day its value as a center of undergraduate and alumnae activities, thus contributing to the growth of a democratic and gracious college spirit.

Marion Gaylord Atwell, Class of 1879; keen student of national and international affairs; gifted with power to observe, inspire and organize; at every period, using her talents and influence for the advantage of her Alma Mater; as President of the New York Club, during whose régime funds were raised for Mary Brigham Hall; as Alumnae Trustee and President of the Alumnae Association making notable contribution to the building of the new Mount Holyoke.

Elizabeth Bartlett Barry, Class of 1881; adding to the prestige of the College as President of the New York Club; as member of the Board of Trustees; a wise and loyal daughter of Mount Holyoke, making the interests of the College her own; responding to every call of her Alma Mater with unmeasured generosity.

MARY LOUISA MATTHEWS, Class of 1884; one of the many representing Mount Holyoke in foreign fields; performing difficult tasks in
dangerous places; as a soldier of Christ fighting with the weapons
which He gave, "the light and truth and love of heaven," in this
way showing forth the ideal of service held by the Founder of the
College.

MARY PHYLINDA DOLE, Class of 1886; ever busy with "works of labor
or of skill" which benefit her Alma Mater, whether as member of
the Board of Trustees of Mount Holyoke or as constant supporter of
Alumnae Clubs; whose knowledge of the fine old art of weaving is
devoted to establishing a fund at the College, available for research
in medical science.

FLORENCE PURINGTON, Class of 1886; Treasurer, Dean, Trustee; associated with the College from graduation to the present hour; in
every post a wise counselor, inspiring confidence and preserving
loyalty among alumnae in all parts of the world.

MARY WARNER CROWELL, Class of 1889; revealing in her performance
of the duties of Alumnae Secretary the attention to detail and re-
sourcefulness requisite for success, to whose spirit of enterprise is
owing the *Alumnae Quarterly*, official organ of the Alumnae Association for twenty years.

CAROLINE B. GREENE, Class of 1889; during forty years Registrar of
the College, maker and searcher of records, a mine of information,
both accurate and valuable, whose riches have been in daily use.

BERTHA ELIZA BLAKELY, Class of 1893; Librarian of the College since
eighteen hundred ninety-five, efficiently serving the community in
a complex task; quietly communicating to students a love for
books; builder of the new library whose charm and comfort are due
to her foresight and imagination.

BETH BRADFORD GILCHRIST, Class of 1902; author of *The Life of
Mary Lyon*, a valuable interpretation of the true spirit of Mary
Lyon, presenting in its day to a forgetful public the great story of
a great woman, a book that has constantly contributed to the
prestige of Mount Holyoke College.

CHARLOTTE LEAVITT GILPATRIC, Class of 1902; who by her knowledge of means to secure desired ends has rendered distinguished
service to her College; especially as a member of the Seven College
Committee appointed to make the needs and accomplishments of
colleges for women more widely known, has she increased the influence of her Alma Mater.

MARY AUGUSTA CLARK, Class of 1903; endowed by nature with a fine
social conscience, trained to meet social needs, rendering valuable

service to graduates seeking positions, to them and to many others she has given of her resources and of her experience; to all a wise and unfailing friend.

SARAH STREETER LESTER, Class of 1911; whose enthusiastic support of the College is ever an inspiration; the giver of the Sarah Streeter Cup awarded each year to the senior excelling in physical development, thus emphasizing the ideal of Mount Holyoke from its foundation, "The sound mind in the sound body."

CENTENNIAL GIFTS OF THE ALUMNAE

Mrs. White then announced the Centennial Gifts from alumnae. As she read the long list of classes with the amount contributed by each a banner of silver and blue was slowly unrolled at the side of the stage until it reached the proscenium arch and displayed to the entire audience the figures recorded. A similar ceremony with a roll on the other side of the stage accompanied the reading of the lists of gifts from Mount Holyoke Clubs in many communities both in America and abroad. The statement of totals will be found on page 144.

MRS. WHITE: We have had a telegram sent to Miss Mary Warren, our oldest living graduate, of the Class of 1860. It reads:

Affectionate greetings from Mount Holyoke Centenary to the oldest living graduate.

After the singing of *Alma Mater*, the Alumnae Symposium adjourned.

ALUMNAE LUNCHEON

The Alumnae Luncheon at twelve-thirty o'clock on Friday brought together twelve hundred alumnae in the big khaki tent, sixty by one hundred and seventy feet, south of Student-Alumnae Hall, where hundreds of small tables were attractively set and grouped by classes. At the head table were Mrs. White, Miss Woolley, Mrs. Beard, and the other speakers of the morning, Mrs. Lyman, Miss Monchow, and Miss Perkins. After a delicious luncheon, promptly at two o'clock as arranged with the broadcasting companies, Mrs. White rose to present Miss Woolley. Miss Woolley then introduced Mrs. Mary R. Beard, historian, who brought the Alumnae Symposium to a dramatic close in her address The Direction of Women's Education.

PRESIDENT WOOLLEY: Many times I have had the pleasure of greeting the alumnae but never before so large a group or on so significant an occasion. It gives me great joy to welcome you —that goes without saying!

I am glad that at this time, so full of significance, you wish something more than a *festa*, are eager to have an inspiration that will give food for thought in the days to come. What is the meaning of this day that we celebrate? Of the work of Mary Lyon one hundred years ago? Of the opening of higher education to women?

There is no one to whose discussion of these questions we can turn with more confidence than to our special guest of honor and speaker. It gives me keen pleasure to introduce Mrs. Mary Beard.

THE DIRECTION OF WOMEN'S EDUCATION

MARY RITTER BEARD
Historian

Every centenary, however prideful in its review, through its very review compels an appraisal. Indeed praise itself is appraisal. What is called up out of the past on this New England campus, for instance, represents values in the mind of the person who remembers any thing or many things. And even a researcher delving into the unknown for information about the past on this New England campus looks for things deemed valuable at the outset or has the attention arrested during the exploration by matters which appeal to values already in mind. Since all that has taken place on this campus has its setting in space and time, the appraisal involves comparisons and contrasts whatever the competence, brilliance and vitality displayed here.

But this would certainly be a trite comment on this celebration at Mount Holyoke in the year 1937 were it not for the popular belief that Mary Lyon, one hundred years ago, in this new world of America, pioneered in the establishment of equal education for women. Nor is such a belief popular only. It prevails among distinguished specialists in our seats of the highest learning and finds constant expression there in fateful ways. For example, in a recent pamphlet entitled *Learning for Ladies*, an outstanding professor of our day writes as follows:

No emancipation of the human spirit from custom and authority has been without a struggle, and none has made continued headway without the alliance of favorable social and economic forces. Women's increasing participation in educational opportunities and cultural values is a story full of heroism, sacrifices, and militant struggles against both derision and stubborn opposition. America may rightly claim to have been a pioneer in this crusade. It is, in fact, hardly too much to say that, in broadening and deepening the opportunities for girls to enjoy things of the mind, America has made one of her greatest contributions in the age-long contest for human rights.

Beautifully stated, is it not? And yet gratifying as it is to American pride, this presentation of the case does not correspond with historic events and it carries implications that lead to a profound misconception of education and of women's relation to the subject matter and the process. Consider the substance and the upshot of these implications. There is a distinct thing called education—a unit complete in itself. Men created the body, or unit, of knowledge, thought, values and methods called education. It was long in their exclusive guardianship. America pioneered in giving women equal access to this masculine creation and heritage. The great prize has been won at last. Consequently, it is not incumbent upon women to criticize ungratefully this education so lavishly opened to them now; any one who has received it in any institution of learning on the accredited list is fully competent to instruct them; whatever is handed out to them in the guise of education is to be accepted by them as the true substance and sum of education; when they have received it, they are to regard their minds as trained; and there is nothing more to be done unless perchance they wish to hand it on to others in the form of adult education. In short the history of the business is closed like Goethe's book with seven seals. The victory is good. There is really nothing left but to crown the heroes and heroines with laurels and sing in unison: "Peace on earth; goodwill to men."

But in my opinion this conception of what has happened in America and woman's education does not square with the facts. Indeed in all the ledger of American illusions there seems to me to be none more untenable as history, more provincial in outlook, so inconsistent with the total experience of mankind. In part it must be charged to the desire of Protestants to break with the past as error. In part it must be charged to the exigencies of the woman's rights movement which likewise made the past all a wretched mistake.

Of course no illusion is a sound basis for a value-judgment and as a working hypothesis this particular fancy is a perilous one for women. Hence it is important for us to consider what Mary Lyon actually did a century ago in America. Granted that she was a crusading educator, where lay her goal? Of what culture did she propose to make education for women an agency? What culture did her enterprise reflect? We may say, with confidence I believe, that what Mary Lyon actually did a hundred years ago in America was to promote education, within a seminary, for girls of the lower economic brackets representing a class then deemed the bulwark of this republic, on the basis of a Protestant ideology, inspired with a zest for missionary effort including the urge toward charitable work of a Christian temper. Unquestionably this was in the nature of an innovation. Just as unquestionably it mirrored the culture of her day and habitation when, from tiny villages in New

England, Protestants, following in the wake of European Catholic missionaries, were setting forth to convert the "heathen" of the world and stimulate them to humane undertakings. In aspiring to train young women for American life, Mary Lyon also aspired to train missionaries.

How well the missionary effort succeeded was demonstrated for me a few years ago when I visited a woman's Christian college in Japan; there I heard Mary Lyon's name spoken with reverence as we speak it here today with reverence; there I saw a remarkably faithful reproduction of the Protestant humanistic education given by Mary Lyon to girls of the humbler social classes, for the students in the Japanese institution were likewise of those classes.

But what Mary Lyon did not do and could not do was to pioneer in equal education for women. And the truth is that no one ever "pioneers in increasing opportunities and participation." The juxtaposition of those words is meaningless. And actually women had always shared in the prevalent education of races, nations, and classes and in fixing as well as enjoying cultural values. Like the Japanese men, the Japanese women had been trained in feudal practices and Buddhistic philosophy before they began to get Catholic and Protestant indoctrinations and classical economics. With high determination and steadfast courage, Japanese women who had been equally educated responded to the social crisis brought on through our aggressive Commodore Perry's naval coercion; they founded schools for native girls with a view to helping them make the transition from feudalism to commercialism as safely and sanely as possible. Buddhist women thus directed women's education in the reconstruction era of the nineteenth century in Japan. Over one institution which I visited a woman trained in Confucian ethics presided—another educated woman of the old régime. In the ancient flowing Chinese calligraphy, she wrote for me a poem expressing her delight at meeting a person out of the Occident who sat in darkness with respect to Confucius but who was amenable to light, especially to light upon the Confucian doctrine of the family as the basis of a stable society. In the public leadership of such women lay security for all Japan to no small degree. That Japan escaped ruin under the impact of Western commercial and naval power was due in no slight measure to the intelligence and initiative of educated native women hitherto out of touch with the Occident.

How could any American ever have supposed that any economic, political, social or intellectual scheme could have rooted itself in any land without the consent and co-operation of women? Throughout the ages of human societies, even before the founding of colonies in the New World, women had shared in the substance of education devised for and reflecting their class whatever it was. From time to time women were also spurs to new forms of education deemed by them more suitable than the training à la mode. Thus women in pagan Rome, charmed by Hellenic culture, were active agents in Hellenizing themselves and Roman men who had often had no training except that of the barracks and the battlefield. Hellenization meant a training in the liberal arts—the idea of which we ourselves derive from the Greeks through the Romans. Roman women later turned with similar interest and energy to the Christian faith and culture, bestowed their patronage upon holy men of that religion, helped to determine the brand of Christianity which was to prevail in Rome and to finance the early organization of the Church. Beneath the glamor of papal authority regularly lay the power of women's wealth and the strength of their Christian education and loyalty. Christian women, moreover, were direct co-educators of men and women in the Middle Ages. Twelve hundred years before Mount Holyoke began to educate American girls in an institution, in the seventh century to be exact, the Abbess of Whitby on the English frontier was guiding the education of both sexes in the Catholic institution over which she presided; five bishops were there trained by her to teach the new religion and prepare more teachers in their dioceses. Thus after the Roman Empire started on its downward course, the education of Europe by Christian women, as by Christian men, started on its upward swing. For countless women, Christianity and monasticism provided adventures into education.

The same thing was true in the age of the pagan revival. Dissatisfied with theology and eager for a new humanism, European women began in Italy to adventure with the reviving and disseminating of Greek and Roman learning. Discovering the fascinations of natural philosophy no less perhaps than the sensuality of Homer, the very nuns in a convent at Ripoli, equipped with the newly-invented printing-press gadget, issued volume after volume of pre-Christian literature. While militant husbands were away from home on fighting bouts, wives in castles turned to the classics and invited to their halls the leading poets, painters, teachers and writers of the Renaissance inclination. Women monarchs assisted. If Isabella of Spain was "the last of the crusaders," she was the first to adopt the revival of learning and subject her court and the university to its influence; she imported Italian men and women with that intention. In the following century Queen Elizabeth bent over the books of the ancients and was the first of the great English monarchs to adopt the Renaissance. In the seventeenth century, at Lyons, French women of the bourgeoisie met Italian women and together they communed over the classics.

Naturally the court jester, Molière, enchanted the French king and his entourage with his skits on ladies aspiring to such learning but that did not signify that ladies had never before aspired to such learning. Had they not once spoken and written Greek and Latin as their natural tongues? Nor did his scorn suppress the ladies of his time. The education which they espoused steadily advanced against the education of the barracks and the battlefield, which, supreme at court, led the France of the Grand Monarch to the verge of ruin. But early in the nineteenth century an effective blow was delivered to the classics by Mme. de Staël who had studied them with acumen as well as devotion. Aware though she was of the heights to which Greek thought had reached, in a treatise on its limitations she took her stand with the creative force just formulated as The Idea of Progress and emphasized the potentialities of the new science as an agency of culture. In so doing she was not throwing her sex overboard, however, for that science had been built up as a household enterprise for the most part—a traditional practice exemplified in the case of Peter and Marie Curie who kept it up even in the era of the great public laboratories.

This is not to say that women's share in the enjoyment of "things of the mind" and the fixing of cultural values was confined to the convent, the salon, or the simple household prior to the American adventure in college education for women. In the numerous and creative schools of Greek philosophy, women were participants in the effort to think rationally and clearly and comprehensively. They aided in the creation of the very idea of ideas, developing into an idea of education. Over an important academy at Megara the woman, Euklides, presided, with men enrolled under her as students. By the bedside of Socrates just before he drank the hemlock forced upon him by the State were women as well as men philosophers and Socrates like other Greek men freely and naturally acknowledged intellectual borrowings from women. Greek women in the Hellenic age carried Greek culture to the periphery of Roman power. At Alexandria, Hypatia taught mathematics and neo-Platonism and to her lectures male students flocked from near and far. After the Roman imperial collapse when Italian universities rose upon the scene, women both taught and studied there—with distinction; Germans and others in the backwoods offered them teaching posts in order to catch up with Italian culture. From the Middle Ages to our own age, it seems, women have retained the right to attend the universities in the Latin countries of Europe and if more men than women have attended and taught there the explanation does not lie in any bill of exclusion.

Moreover if we inquire where the business of education really started, we encounter primitive women—the prehistoric mothers who made the original human culture by sharply divorcing the human from the brute through their invention of industrial arts and the pursuit of them at the hearth. Women steadily made their culture so acceptable to their mates, engaged in the kill like the animals about them, that eventually man's place like woman's was in the home. Among the Pythagoreans—a great teaching sect in Asia Minor in the sixth century B.C. made up of men and women—living was exalted to the perfection of harmony; food, clothing, song, dance, gesture, mood and mind were deliberately drawn together for the objective of peace and beauty. If the original education—the true pioneering—was in the fundamental humanities and feminine in inspiration, in the liberal arts, the arts of peace, it is inconceivable that the last education can be far removed from the fundamental humanities.

No doubt as we turn to the thought of today, we remember that women were shut out of Anglo-Saxon universities. But education in England did not all occur in universities, and the educators and students there assembled were not always devoted to the enrichment and dissemination of learning. According to Edward Gibbon's account of Oxford, as late as the eighteenth century they were little concerned with education.

The Fellows or monks of my time [says Gibbon] were decent, easy men, who supinely enjoyed the gifts of the founder: their days were filled by a series of uniform employments—the chapel, the hall, the coffee-house and the common-room—till they retired weary and well satisfied to a long slumber. From the toil of reading, writing or thinking they had absolved their consciences. Their conversation stagnated in a round of college business, Tory politics, personal anecdotes and private scandal.

Were not innumerable English women, deprived of equality in that game, doing better for themselves? Though Mary Astell lamented the loss of Catholic equalities in education and tried to secure Protestant equalities against the opposition of

Bishop Burnet, her own training was of the best in England; it included the study of Latin, logic, and mathematics under the direction of a learned uncle. Certainly no man had written more skilfully on that crucial chapter of English history, the revolutionary movement of the Puritan age, than Lucy Hutchinson in her Memoir of her husband, Colonel Hutchinson. And she was matched in the new world later by Mercy Warren who displayed literary power, insight and critical political judgment in her three-volumed *History of the American Revolution*. While Abigail Adams like Mary Astell yearned to have her sex better educated, Abigail Adams like Mary Astell must be acknowledged as a substantially educated woman of the century in which she lived and asserted rebellious leadership. Her letters during the Revolution and afterwards from England compare well with any letters written from Massachusetts or England by men and women in the twentieth century decorated with college degrees.

The broad view and the long view of education therefore seem to lead alike to the conclusion that America did not exactly pioneer in opening educational opportunities to women. In the age of Catholic unity and in Latin countries, women had enjoyed educational opportunities of many kinds. Where the doors of formal institutions had been barred to women, they had managed to acquire an education in other ways. Though Harvard, Yale and Princeton were closed to American women in the Protestant age, the women of the American Revolution were without a doubt not only indispensable to the triumph of economic independence but were also independent and forceful thinkers.

That illiteracy was not the common lot of white women in America before the day of equal opportunity in formal education is made evident by the early surveys of the Census. The first survey, taken in 1840, shows that slightly over 90 per cent of the white men and women twenty years of age and older could read and write. Although the next Census taken in 1850 reveals a small drop, still 90 per cent of the native white population could read and write. When deficiencies in opportunity are considered, the relative education of women is amazing. In seven states there were more illiterate men than women and out of a total in round numbers of 936,000 illiterate whites the excess of illiterate women over illiterate men was only 183,000 in round numbers. In respect of the Latin tradition to which I have referred, it is interesting to note that among the whites in New Mexico in 1850 the number of illiterate men exceeded the number of illiterate women. It would be improper to make these figures mean too much but they surely dispose of the fiction that women were far behind men in literacy in 1837 when presumably the pioneering in equal education began. In adopting the illusion that they had been nothing with respect to education, in cutting loose from their own vast heritage of knowledge, experience, and thought, in casting off the ennobling memory of themselves, women lost their bearings as women and therefore as human beings all of whom are either men or women. Thus when the doors of institutions of formal learning were unlocked for them, they too lightly accepted as education the body of knowledge and the developing doctrines which the masters of those institutions deemed to be education in its fulness.

This terrific break in woman's tradition may be illustrated by a single example although a large comprehension of its significance can only come from an intimate acquaintance with the archives of women—that is, with the speeches and writings of the hundreds of American women who in the middle period of American history were public personalities. The single illustration I have selected is afforded by the thought of Elizabeth Cady Stanton with reference to American democracy and civilization. Despite her lack of a Harvard, Yale, Princeton or Columbia degree, this mother of many sons accustomed to ask her basic questions about history, nations, government and law, replied to them out of a wide and deep knowledge illuminated by her humanist sympathies. For many years two o'clock in the morning was her regular bedtime and the intervening hours were spent in reading the opinions of the wise and turning these over in the alembic of her own intelligence. What was produced in her own mind was given to the public, from the platform, over a period of twelve years and more, during eight months annually, as she toured the continent under the auspices of the Lyceum bureau. As early as 1868, when the Proclamation of Emancipation for which she had worked so hard was still on every tongue, Mrs. Stanton, by no means a tired radical, turned her face to the future and said to a great audience this thing:

A knowledge of the history of the past teaches us that the law governing all human affairs is change, progress, development in the world of thought as well as action . . . A healthy discontent is the first step of progress . . . In the long battle we have fought in this country for the emancipation and enfranchisement of the African race, the principles of slavery and freedom have been so fully described that it does not require much discrimination to see that the condition of the laboring masses in the North differs little from that of the colored race under the old system on the plantations of the South . . . I ask those in the full enjoyment of all the blessings which wealth can give to look around in the filthy lanes and bystreets of all our cities, [into the factories and workshops, into the furnaces and mines]. Those who believe that poverty is a divine plan will consider their duty done in the manifestation of sympathy and charity. But for those who believe it is the result of human ignorance and selfishness and can be remedied, a widely different course of action must be pursued. To the last class I belong.

This attitude and this spirit were the attitude and the spirit of a large body of women at that time who were intensely concerned with social principles, with the distribution of wealth as a principle of culture, and with the good life. They had a strong desire to be good citizens and to promote good citizenship.

The break in that feminine tradition of concern with social principles came with college education for women. In the formal instruction which girls began to receive in the sixties and which led in the eighties to the elevation of Mount Holyoke from a seminary to the status of a college, the controlling influence, aside perhaps from the courses in belles lettres, was the secular, amoral, materialistic, mechanistic doctrine of each against all, sometimes described in a daintier fashion as laissez faire. William Graham Sumner expounded this doctrine to the men at Yale and his disciples expounded it to women blessed with an equal education. J. Laurence Laughlin expatiated upon the doctrine of anarchy checked only by the policeman, acquisition and selfish enjoyment, greed and citizen irresponsibility, first at Harvard and then at the University of Chicago; thence it was spread to other colleges as truth, science, law and the gospel. This creed regnant upon American campuses in the era of equal college education in the so-called "humanities" denied the rôle and force of interests in society, left the power of property out of its reckoning, and offered nature in the raw, freed even from the interests and unions of class, as the foundation of life and labor, of humanity, of civilization and culture. Other points of view, older points of view, became mere "sentimental twaddle" conducive to debilitating "effeminacy." If any young woman on a college campus argued that all economic and political activities spring from social and moral interests, as the founding fathers and mothers of our democratic republic had formerly argued, her voice was drowned out by the thunders of the schoolmen and school administrations in the early days of equal collegiate education.

Hence in the process of oral instruction and textbooks on American campuses through which amoral and mechanistic, insensate, laissez-faire indoctrinated the education of women, one of the strangest pages in their history was shaped. A few details point the amoral. In 1884 Professor Laughlin published an edition of John Stuart Mill's *Political Economy* which became the authoritative text. In this edition he reduced the enlightened individualism of Mill to the level of a sheer animal struggle for existence. He claimed to have simplified Mill but in reality he mutilated Mill by cutting out all his humanism and retaining every defense of greed. He even added passages which Mill would have spurned as thoroughly ignoble. This meant casting out the feminine tradition in a peculiar way for Mill had boldly confessed that his departure from the narrowness and inadequacies of classical economy was due to the recognition of the relevant humanism which his wife, an outstanding English feminist, had brought to his attention and demonstrated to be a vital part of any all-inclusive thought about political economy. This also meant casting out Mill's whole chapter on the prospects of labor in which Mill had advocated equal opportunities coupled with equal responsibilities for women. Thus by one of the major ironies of history, an American professor shattered for American women, formally educated in the eighties and the nineties, the intellectual and moral nexus that had bound them to the self-educated women of the Enlightenment. Not only that. Formal education now gave them an education in economics and behavior that was neither true nor real nor intellectually honest.

Moreover while Sumner, the theologian turned academician, and Laughlin, a former president of the Manufacturers' Fire Insurance Company, likewise turned academician, were initiating young men and women, equally educated, into the mysteries of what was now classed as "economic and political science," historians were inculcating in them a corresponding idea of human history. Thus at Chicago University, Professor von Holst held forth on history, in a manner identical with the manner of the political economist in a neighboring classroom, as both fitted the atmosphere of the neighboring stockyards where nature in the raw was so vigorously demonstrated. For instance during the Pullman strike, von Holst condemned organized labor as organized crime and, drawing up historical batteries against any humanistic plan for human relations, he repeated Napoleon's dictum that shooting a thousand men is often in the end the best way to avoid shooting thousands of men.

Meanwhile the tooth-and-claw philosophy of Darwin and Spencer, brought across the Atlantic as learning, was taught to young Americans of both sexes as biological necessity opposed to humane sentiments and actual practices in mutual aid. The extension of tooth and claw to international relations—a thing which Mill had rejected—was now defended on American campuses as an extension of the principle ruling national life and labor—the war of each against all. But if this rule had been fully applied when learned, hungry mothers would have snatched the last crumb of bread from their babies, feminists would have become unqualified Amazons, and trade union leaders and sympathizers would have put aside all collective bargaining in favor of the weapons which the newest educators of history praised so highly—the weapons of tooth and claw making all life and labor red with blood. *Homo homini lupus.* As far as the rule was accepted by women, it tended to become an awful boomerang, in times of financial panic, for what was fair in such a social war was fair for them as human beings thus visualized.

In other words, that formal education to which women had won access and which was said to be such a blessing repudiated and condemned every humane tradition of the education which had been woman's heritage from the Enlightenment. Fortunately, by the time women had been thoroughly imbued with the new learning, that very learning began to be understood as a hollow mockery of life. It was so one-sided as to be untrue. It was so unreal as to be false in letter and in social temper. Just as women had proved that they were able to carry the full college program to which the pioneers had won access, its presuppositions and assurances blew up in their faces. Laissez faire did not operate in practice all round as the professors had prophesied and, where it did, the conjuncture of plutocracy, urban poverty and farm tenancy could not be universally regarded as fulfilling the promise of American life so defined on the campuses. So the reappearance of the humanism of the Enlightenment forced a reconsideration of all education, even for men, and of the social policy of which education is phase.

In this American renaissance and revision, a noted triumvirate of college alumnae living in Chicago—Jane Addams, Julia Lathrop, and Florence Kelley—in the very center of individualistic political economy, history, biology and sociology calling itself science, revived the feminine tradition and accepting the fact that they were women, though equally educated, offered society and its educational institutions a philosophy and learning less in conformity with the stockyards. With Professors Richard T. Ely and John R. Commons, themselves not subdued to the concept of liberty as unrestrained license, these collegiate alumnae took leadership in a vigorous campaign for thought and action better conceived. Within a short span of years they helped to write ethical gains into legislation and transform the outlook of American education for men no less than for women. This they did by going outside the academic cloister, by recognizing other life than that in dormitories, by remaining true to their own experiences and reasoning, by maintaining close contact with the realities of the common life —in short, by insisting upon that realism which is in fact the essence of the scientific spirit.

It was in harmony with this American renaissance and revision that Mary E. Woolley began to direct the education of girls as President of Mount Holyoke at the turn of our own century—a tendency that bridged the chasm cut by laissez faire in the Enlightenment. The new spirit had already begun to clear up the imperative of academic dogmatism and reconstruct the essential contact with the common life. For President Woolley the college was never a mere cloister for refining ancient theories or splitting hairs inordinately split in times past. That was never her idea of a liberal arts course. Through membership and activity in numerous civic societies, ranging from the League for Permanent Peace to the American Association for Labor Legislation, she faced great public issues in their insistent forms. She encouraged her faculty to keep their windows open upon the wide world. She tried to remove the barriers between learning and living, accepting for herself grave obligations imposed upon her by the President of the United States and recognizing the truth that the leader in education must bear the hazardous but challenging responsibilities of a public personality. In speaking for American culture, President Woolley has not spoken merely for a class endowed with special privileges justifying the exploitation of other classes. For her, education is related to the needs of society; of humanity at large now struggling in times dark and confused for a policy designed to procure for men and women human rights, human dignity, and security, amid the insensate pressure for a retreat to barbarism. The heritage of her spirit she bequeathes to her successors and to the alumnae of her college who, in cherishing this institution and education for women must, if they are loyal to their own intelligence and to this trust, widen their sympathies to the very borders of society and seek knowledge for society endlessly and without fear.

What happens on this campus is symbolic of happenings in all women's education. It is prophetic of men's fate no less than women's. Any evasion of evident duties would spell cowardice. Such evasion would be a sign of intellectual and moral anaemia —the inertia of life—forecasting death for individuals, for institutions and for society at large. Such an inertia to the point of cowardice would be particularly tragic at this hour when all western civilization has reached a crisis in its economy, in its thought, and in its human relations. The nature of this crisis is ominous in that such prosperity as the world now enjoys synchronizes with mounting expenditures for instruments of human destruction unparalleled in the long and appalling history of mankind.

Before us all indeed is the urgency of an intelligent choice in the direction of women's education. Before us is the choice between the acceptance of sheer force and the rationalization of its emotions which are in the main the masculine historic inclination, and the humanism of enlightenment with the power of intuitive insight into moral and esthetic values which are in the main the historic feminine inclination. It is the choice once more between the barracks, the battlefield, the concentration camp, soldier-breeding and cloistral scholasticism on the one side; and the home, the arts of peaceful industry, training for life, and the exchange of cultural values on the other side. With good reason do Nietzsche and Bäumler and all their affiliates make women the eternal enemy of the military state.

In the choice which women now make lie the perils of extreme effeminacy no doubt—the preference and quest for ease, comfort and luxury, that is for over-refinement. However, at this hour when the balance is so heavily weighted on the side of militarism and sheer force, the women who know their history and understand their rôle in the processes of a humane civilization can make only one decision. They must cling deliberately and firmly to their principle of history, take their stand for the cause of enlightened humanism, and make their direction of the education of girls serve the ends of that grand cause.

But let there be no misunderstanding of that education. It means no mere instruction in the arts of keeping house, in child psychology, in sex wiles, in marital relations or the technicalities of scholarship and research, however important these may be as subsidiaries. It does mean education based squarely on the feminine principle of history, without surrender to men on the march for the kill, and sensitive to the public responsibilities which inexorably flow from that principle.

The preservation and development of this education is, then, no simple tea party for little women and little men. "In much wisdom there is much grief and he that increaseth knowledge increaseth sorrow." So the preservation and development of women's education is a phase of that eternal conflict between the ideal and the real which now splits western civilization to the bottom of its heart. It is a phase of that everlasting struggle for the maintenance and enlargement of those enduring values, the cohesive forces of society, which alone make possible the opportunities in education, economy and culture for all men and women of goodwill.

Woman *is* and *makes* history. *Sub specie aeternitatis.*

DEPARTMENTAL EXHIBITS

At the close of the Alumnae Luncheon, the guests of Mount Holyoke dispersed to find entertainment or rest, according to their individual tastes. By this time the sun was shining on a campus which showed all the loveliness of New England in spring—the soft green of newly opened leaves, the cloudy pink of apple blossoms in the orchard, the brilliant colors of tulips in the formal garden.

On both Friday and Saturday afternoons it was possible for guests to visit any of the exhibits provided by the several departments of the College. The static exhibits were also open at other hours. The combined College Choirs gave a program of music in Mary Lyon Chapel under the direction of Dr. William Churchill Hammond and consisting largely of music composed or arranged by Clara Tillinghast, the organist, and a Mount Holyoke graduate of the Class of 1902. The Department of English Literature and Drama presented, in the Laboratory Theatre, "The Vest Pocket Standby," a play written, during her undergraduate days, by Eleanore Price of the Class of 1932. The program was appropriately dedicated to Miss Woolley. The Art Department had arranged an exhibition of works of art by Mount Holyoke alumnae and members of the faculty, numbering 102 items, an exhibit which remained in the galleries of Dwight Art Memorial until June the eighteenth. Other departments had arranged exhibits of scientific or artistic material or of students' work, which ranged all the way from archeological specimens of the Stone Age to choral speaking demonstrations and from a "chemistry class of 1840" enacted by students of the Chemistry Department, to demonstrations of laboratory experiments and techniques of today in other science departments. Programs for these exhibits are printed in the Appendix on pages 169–181.

Among the most interesting and valuable was the exhibit in the Treasure Room of Williston Memorial Library, prepared under the direction of Miss Flora B. Ludington, Librarian. One Hundred American First Editions, paralleling year by year the History of Mount Holyoke College, had been brought together from the library's own treasures and through loans of rare volumes from other libraries and private collections. The procession began with Emerson's *American Scholar* (1837) and closed with Van Wyck Brooks' *The Flowering of New England* (1936) and included such noteworthy first editions as *The Raven* (1845), *Uncle Tom's Cabin* (1852), *Leaves of Grass* (1855), *The Gettysburg Address* (1863), and *The Education of Henry Adams* (1907). The manuscript accompanying Mary Lyon's *A Missionary Offering* (1843) attracted much attention. The fifteen hundred Centennial guests were followed by many more during the remaining days in May, some of them drawn by the favorable notices the exhibition catalogue had received in literary columns of the press. Included in it were an introduction by Van Wyck Brooks, a chronology of Mount Holyoke history, and for each of the one hundred books a descriptive or critical note written by some member of the faculty.

Other library exhibitions were arranged in the Whiting Alcove and the Assembly Hall, illustrating the history of Mount Holyoke. Here were seen volumes of manuscript letters of Mary Lyon, minutes of the first committee meetings at Ipswich during the inception of the new Seminary, the records of subscriptions to the project, and a long series of journal letters begun in 1843. Prospectuses and catalogues of earlier schools with which Mary Lyon was connected as pupil or teacher, along with early catalogues of Mount Holyoke, anniversary addresses and biographies of Mary Lyon, indicated the status of female education

MARY LYON AND REVEREND MR. CONDIT

Represented by Alice N. Wiley, Class of 1938, and
Reverend Henry David Gray of South Hadley

THE ALUMNAE MEDAL OF HONOR

a century ago. The textbook collection suggested not only Mount Holyoke's curriculum, but the methods used and the content of instruction given to students of both sexes in the Seminary period. Over two thousand publications by former students and by present members of the faculty disclosed the breadth of intellectual interest of Mount Holyoke during the hundred years.

HISTORICAL PANTOMIME

At four-thirty and at five-fifteen on Friday audiences gathered on the lawn before a Brigham Hall slightly altered to suggest the original Seminary building. The threatening thunderstorm waited; and Mount Holyoke people of a century ago, impersonated by students, faculty members, and townspeople, enacted a pantomime of the opening day.

MOUNT HOLYOKE OPENS

By SYDNEY R. McLEAN

Under the auspices of the

DRAMATIC CLUB OF MOUNT HOLYOKE COLLEGE

HELEN P. WHEELER, Chairman of Production
HELEN W. CURRIE, Director

The action of *Mount Holyoke Opens* is based on records in the possession of the College, but dramatic purposes have dictated certain compromises with history.

SCENE. Exterior of the first Seminary building.

TIME. Mid-afternoon, Wednesday, November 8, 1837.

FOREWORD. This is the long awaited opening day. Students have been arriving for the past few days, and more are to come. A year and a month ago the corner stone to the building was laid, but shortage of funds—the country is in a state of business depression—have held operations back. Now, however, November eighth is here.

But the building is not yet in order. Just this morning the steps to the front piazza were put in place by carpenters, aided by Deacon Porter. One of the two student parlors is furnished, thanksto money contributed by students of Wheaton Seminary, who have surrendered their principal, Miss Caldwell, to the new institution, for she had promised to come to Mount Holyoke on its opening. Deacon Safford is tacking down matting on the platform in Seminary Hall. Some furniture is not yet delivered, but the townspeople—South Hadley has been generous in giving to the Seminary, both money and labor—are bringing it as it comes and setting it up. Certain students are bringing linen from their home towns, for Miss Lyon has appealed to sewing circles for donations.

Students work to put the building in order, side by side with teachers, townspeople, trustees, and trustees' wives. There are no servants at Mount Holyoke in 1837; every young lady expects to do her share of the housework, and is glad to, because her fee for tuition and board is therefore to be only sixty-four dollars a year. Students enter into the work willingly; they are the daughters of "well bred families," and as such are versed in housekeeping lore.

More have applied for entrance than can be admitted; there are accommodations for only eighty. A few come who fail the examinations and must depart. Mount Holyoke is a literary institution for young ladies over sixteen years of age. It has been endowed by the people, and is a great experiment: the first seminary for the higher education of women so endowed for permanence.

Synopsis. Louisa, Sophronia, and Augusta are carrying boxes to the basement, taking a roundabout route instead of going through the house because there is much activity within doors. Harriet, Serena, and Bethiah are exploring the grounds, though Serena improves her time with a book. Cordelia from the upper piazza calls them to help her and they hurry in.

Nancy and Theresa are on the upper piazza as a wagon drives up the road. They look down, watching as Miranda, Almira, and Rachel, eager to help if needed, run toward the wagon. Dr. Dwight and John have brought some furniture. As John walks along the path, Nancy leans over the railing; John sees her, and after an instant of hesitation proceeds on his way. Deacon Safford, who has appeared with Miss Caldwell, helps John; and after the wagon is empty, Dr. Dwight, who is a busy man, drives off.

John has not seen the last of Nancy. As he emerges for the final load he finds her on the piazza. Ostensibly she has come for a chair, but she knows—as does Theresa, who disapproves—that she wants to see him once more. They enter the building together.

Now a surrey comes along the road, with five tired passengers, who have made the journey from Vermont in three days. The girls climb down, but Martha, after one glance at the bleak building, decides that she is homesick.

Her sister, Catherine, and her friends, Sarah and Frances, are bolder and go up the steps, there to be greeted by Miss Lyon and Miss Caldwell, who have come to the piazza. Martha, after an inner struggle and some reassurance from friendly Deacon Safford, makes up her mind to remain; and when she is welcomed by Miss Lyon she is glad. She follows the others inside, as her father takes the trunks around to the side entrance.

Mrs. Safford and Mrs. Porter, grateful for a rest from their self-imposed housekeeping tasks, come to the road, waiting for Deacon Porter, who has driven with a friend into the countryside on an errand. The ladies are accompanied by Abigail Moore, Miss Lyon's niece, who is a senior this first year. She has left the seminary in Virginia which she has headed for three years to come to Mount Holyoke. Mrs. Porter is anxious to see her husband, for she has found certain carpentry details that need correction, and he, as chairman of the building committee, must attend to them. He arrives with his friend, who drives off immediately. The group start for the building, when they are halted by another arrival.

Zeviah, her father, and another gentleman have driven from their home town with a box of linen sent by the ladies of the church. The box is large, and her father needs help in lifting it, so Zeviah impulsively hails Deacon Porter. He is glad to aid, and so is young Byron Smith, the village boy who acts as Miss Lyon's messenger and who emerges to see what is going on now. News of the arrival reaches the house, and the teachers come to unpack the box, for it is too large to go through the doorway. Miss Lyon is grateful for this additional evidence that people are supporting the Seminary.

Still further evidence is ahead. Miss Lyon sees Mr. and Mrs. Hawks approaching from the village and waits for them with the deacons, as others carry the linen indoors. Mr. Hawks, who has for nearly three years been financial agent, turns over some money he has just collected, and Miss Lyon gives it to Deacon Porter, good business man that he is.

And then comes the stagecoach. Byron runs to the road excitedly; Miss Lyon and Miss Hodgman, who has returned—this pretty flirtatious young teacher does not like to miss anything—wait on the piazza as the girls descend from the coach. The driver, the guard, and a passenger—who has been riding outside as gentlemen often prefer to—are interested in the building, and with difficulty the driver and the guard persuade themselves to go about their work of guiding the coach to the side entrance and there unloading bandboxes and trunks. Only Prudence has an escort, her father. The others— Emma, Philena, Elizabeth, Caroline, Persis, and Wealthy—precede her to the piazza, eager and absorbed in their new surroundings; except for Emma, who has taught in a Boston seminary and is sure that Mount Holyoke has nothing new to offer her. She does not know that many of her associates among the student body have, like her, taught before and have come here to perfect their knowledge.

Not so Prudence. She, poor child, is only fifteen, under the required age, but her father has brought her in hope that she will be admitted. She watches her fellow passengers go into the building, and makes her curtsy to Miss Lyon. Then comes disappointment. Miss Lyon asks her age, and when she hears it refuses to accept her. But her father pleads, and Miss Lyon, who is very kind, consents at least to allow an examination. This must be administered on the piazza, for Prudence will not enter the building unless she is to stay. But alas, she is not accepted, for Miss Caldwell, summoned by Miss Hodgman to give the examination, says that she does not pass. So it is fortunate that the stage-coach has not yet gone; Prudence and her father can board it again and go sadly home.

Miss Lyon sends Byron for her Bible; four o'clock is close at hand, the time for the religious services that will mark the official opening. Mr. Condit is to preside, and even now he is on his way from the parsonage. He walks up the steps, and the two consult as to a suitable passage to read, a duty deferred till now because both have been very busy. Mr. Condit takes the Bible and with Byron enters the building. Miss Lyon wishes for a moment to be alone.

She descends the steps and walks along the path. She is very proud of the building, quite conscious of the greatness of the work she and her associates have accomplished during more than three long years of labor and prayer. Here stands the first building of Mount Holyoke, and others will surely follow, for the Seminary is destined to endure from generation to generation.

A bell rings; it is four o'clock, time for the religious services. Miss Lyon walks up the steps, enters the building, and a few minutes later Mount Holyoke opens.

CAST OF CHARACTERS

In order of appearance

Louisa	Mary V. Jacoby
Sophronia	Mary E. Glynn
Augusta	Dorothy Goldstein
Harriet	Mary Anderson
Serena	Eleanor M. Clough
Bethiah	Helen A. Chapman
Cordelia	Ruth C. Andrew
Nancy Everett	Jean S. Quinn
Theresa	Ruth J. Adams
Miranda	Sara M. Gooding
Almira	Mary Elizabeth White

John Dwight, son of Elihu Dwight....................Donald W. Bailey
Dr. Elihu Dwight, South Hadley physician................Asa S. Kinney
Miss Eunice Caldwell, associate principal..................Betty Abbott
Deacon Daniel Safford, of Boston, a trustee...................John Lobb
Martha's father................................Frank E. Bailey, Jr.
Martha..Katharine E. Metcalf
Catherine...Joan H. Beckett
Sarah..Ritamary M. Althouse
Frances...Elizabeth W. Phraner
Miss Mary Lyon.....................................Alice N. Wiley
Mrs. Andrew W. Porter........................F. Elizabeth Tweedle
Mrs. Daniel Safford.................................Jane E. Collins
Abigail Moore.......................................Jane M. Hume
Deacon Andrew W. Porter, of Monson, a trustee.......Leslie G. Burgevin
Deacon Porter's friend.............................Rogers D. Rusk
Zeviah...Emily C. Thompson
Zeviah's father..................................Roger W. Holmes
Gentleman...Herbert Moore
Byron Smith, a South Hadley boy..................Robert H. Matthias
Miss Mary W. Smith, a teacher.....................Constance Hutzler
Miss Amanda A. Hodgman, a teacher...................Louise A. Kerr
The Reverend Roswell Hawks, a trustee and agent in
    collecting funds for the Seminary..................Gerald W. Brace
Mrs. Roswell Hawks.............................Edith M. Albertson
Stagecoach driver..............................Horace T. Brockway
Guard..Stuart M. Stoke
A passenger..Robert Balk
Prudence's father.................................Samuel P. Hayes
Emma..Margaret Garmey
Philena...Emily C. Roberts
Elizabeth.......................................Eleanor M. Griffeth
Caroline..Katharine Irons
Persis..Florence E. Gipe
Wealthy...Rebecca Partridge
Prudence...Janice E. Hallett
The Reverend Joseph D. Condit, pastor of the Congre-
    gational Church of South Hadley and secretary-
    of the Seminary Board of Trustees. The Reverend Henry David Gray

GARDEN PARTY, COURT OF HONOR, AND
CROWNING OF THE FUTURE

On the Pageant Field and in the College Gardens was given a Garden Party on Friday afternoon attended by some five thousand guests. Tables and chairs, shaded by gay umbrellas, scattered about the lawn offered places for rest or conversation. Over three hundred girls in authentic costumes of Mount Holyoke's one hundred years made agreeable and picturesque hostesses who carried the guests back in spirit across the century as the Goldman Band played the old airs that have been favorites of students throughout the years. Sherbet tables at three corners of the field provided refreshment, and in the garden the Class of 1904 with their college daughters presided over another table.

Beneath the north avenue of trees was placed the Court of Honor, where ten "lovely ladies" representing the past ten decades sat or stood talking with favored guests. When the notes of a trumpet sounded from the tower on the hill above, the beloved President of the College appeared in the distance escorted by six of the court ladies and attendants. As they proceeded through the gardens, hundreds of the guests thronged forward to give them welcome.

At the same time the student hostesses left the field, but presently reappeared in procession arranged according to their costumes from 1837 to 1937, the group for each decade curtsying to the President as they passed the Court of Honor. The long lines wound across the field and down to the bridge, there separating for the approach from the hill of the Future Mount Holyoke with her modern Court, seniors chosen for their beauty and grace of face and spirit and charming in the costumes of the present. The Queen of the Court, on arriving before the President, presented her with flowers and was duly crowned. In the face of a storm with thunder, lightning and a downpour of rain, the queen and the ladies of 1837 to 1937 picked up their skirts and fled to shelter with the guests, in-

Holyoke Transcript-Telegram

THE GARDEN

THE COURT OF HONOR IN COSTUMES OF TEN DECADES

THE CANOE PAGEANT

stead of singing the old *Alma Mater* which was planned as the finale.

DANCE RECITAL

The Recital took place at nine o'clock on Friday and Saturday evenings in Chapin Auditorium.

When a dance program for the Centenary celebration was first discussed, it was thought that American Youth would be fitting and proper as subject matter. Further study of this theme made apparent the fact that the problems of youth were those which confronted society as a whole. After much research, and with invaluable help from the Department of History, Marie Heghinian, Assistant Professor in the Department of Physical Education, worked out a historically accurate panorama of American Society as a basis for the dance compositions.

It may be of interest to note that the dance choreography preceded the composition of the music, which was written especially for the cycle.

Although the following program notes can in no way portray the exciting climaxes of the dances, the rhythm and counter rhythm of the music, or the vivid coloring of the costumes, they will in some measure convey the underlying theme of the dance performance.

CHANGING AMERICA

A Dance Cycle

I. RAW EARTH. The call of the New World brought to the shores of America people of hope, vision, and ambition. Many came to find a haven from religious oppression; others planned to found homes in the wilderness; still others were drawn by the magnet of gold. All were filled with the passion to discover, build, and achieve. This passion they left as a heritage to their children.

    1. New World..Group I

II. RICH SOIL. The driving forces of youthful vigor and energy found spontaneous expression in various ways. The pioneers of the Western plains loved and cultivated the soil; the planters of the South established a gracious mode of living which was destroyed by the Civil War; and the adventurers of the far West lived hardily, boisterously, riotously. All of these natural patterns of existence ended with the passing of the frontier.

1. On the Plains....................................Group II

2. Dusk over the South.............................Group III

3. Dance Hall Folic................................Group IV

III. FALSE HARVEST. The youthful drive of the preceding period became a mad rush for material gain, a lust for gold. The consequent mechanization of life and the fierce competition in industry sent men to the cities, where they erected towering skyscrapers as cathedrals for the worship of Mammon. The destruction and dissolution of this evidence of material security temporarily plunged the people into hopelessness and apathy. But through the darkness of despair was ever present the unquenchable spirit of youth.

1. City Streets....................................Group II

2. A Cry in the Land..............................Group III

IV. NEW PLANTING. From the chaos of a society disintegrated through internal conflict may rise a false Messiah, a Dictator, toward whom the people first turn in their despair. But as the pattern of regimentation begins to take form under his iron will, they rise in rebellion and tear him from his pedestal. A regenerated society returns to the simplicity of its early American heritage, but with a new sense of social co-operation which has been momentarily lost in the mad rush of competition. This return is manifest in the triumphant conception of an integrated society.

1. Regimentation..................................Group IV

2. Hymn of Faith..................................Group I

THE DANCERS

GROUP I. Gertrude Adams, Dorothy Califf, Ruth Cronk, Bettie Foote, Thisbe Grieco, Susan Houser, Roslyn Kerney, Marietta Kuolt, Elizabeth Manson, Nancy Mettler, Catherine Rand, Juliet Shaw, Mary Jane Smith, Ruth Spencer, Barbara Streeter, Mildred Thomssen, Janet Watt, Mary Wick, Mary Willett.

GROUP II. Ruth Adams, Susie Burdick, Myrtle Compton, Mary Dolbeare, Kathryn Eisner, Ruth Hagedorn, Constance Hutzler, Barbara Johnson, Alice

Johnston, Phillis Kaler, Marcia Kidder, Charlotte Knapp, Marjorie Mullally, Jane Schaap.

GROUP III. Virginia Anderson, Barbara Banker, Elizabeth Beach, Ann Beckstedt, Janet Gilbert, Pauline Hemp, Marion Ludke, Grace Mangini, Barbara Peck, Eleanor Sayer, Rosemary Shafer, Hope Wells.

GROUP IV. Mildred Black, Jane Burnett, Betty Caulkins, Jeanne Curtis, Katharine Emmel, Emily Gifford, Judith Hammond, Madeline Heckenbleikner, Grace Nelson, Candace Preston, Emily Roberts, Ann Shroyer.

ORCHESTRA

Piano, Norman Lloyd
Flute, Otto Monnard
Clarinet, Robert Klepfer
Clarinet, George Dietz
Trumpet, Leonard Meretta
Percussion, Donald Bonham

Choreography by Marie Heghinian
Music specially composed for The Dance by Norman Lloyd
Costumes by Pauline Lawrence

RECEPTION FOR GUESTS

The Reception for Guests was scheduled to take place on Mandelle Terrace during and after the Dance Recital. The setting would have been ideal; flood lights were to give the effect of soft moonlight, and the Goldman Band was to add the romance of music. Since the weather was not co-operative, President Woolley, Mr. Morrison, President of the Board of Trustees, Dean Allyn, and Dean Cheek, received in the living-room of South Mandelle. A portion of the Goldman Band played during the evening in the South sun-porch. All the public rooms of North and South Mandelle were thrown open to the twenty-five hundred guests in line.

SERENADE AND CANOE PAGEANT

The Serenade and Canoe Pageant, postponed by Jupiter Pluvius until Saturday evening, proved a happy finale to the

Centennial Days. Well-hidden floodlights had turned the shores of Lower Lake into a landscape shimmering and strange. These and other campus illuminations were made possible by the generosity of the General Electric Company. The feathery woods on Prospect were bathed in silver, the leafy banks of the brook in a glimmering green twilight. Along the footbridge and on the shore below Mandelle crowded the dark forms of the spectators.

At ten-twenty-nine an announcer spoke into his microphone —"Stations WBZ and WBZA, testing from Mount Holyoke College." On the dot of ten-thirty a fleet of canoes, their small gauze sails covered with a glittering phosphorescent substance, slipped noiselessly from beneath the Pageant Field bridge. The Freshman Class, watching through the dark the white-gloved hands of the Junior Song Leader, Miss Judith B. Welles of Wethersfield, Connecticut, began their serenade of songs both old and new.

The canoes moved on. As they reached the center of the lake and began their manoeuvres, colored floodlights played from the shore, and the sails shot back sparkles of rose, gold, green, and blue. Station WBZ's broadcast shifted to a commentator on the footbridge, who followed with a running description the silent, kaleidoscopic spectacle of the boats as they formed patterns and figures. From the south end of the shore rose the applause of the audience, from the north, the familiar songs. As the canoes retreated and the announcer closed the broadcast, the Mary Lyon tower clock struck the hour of eleven.

EVENTS OF SATURDAY
MAY THE EIGHTH

THE CENTENARY CEREMONIES

THE Centenary Ceremonies took place on Saturday morning, May the eighth, at ten-thirty o'clock. Because of the clouded skies and chilly air, the preliminary academic procession across the campus was omitted, and the faculty, the official representatives of two hundred and forty-six colleges, universities, and other institutions, the recipients of honorary degrees, and other participants in the ceremonies assembled in Student-Alumnae Hall. Fortunately, however, after the exercises in Chapin Auditorium were over, the skies had cleared so that the academic procession could emerge from the building. The guests, who had earlier been deprived of a view of the dignitaries, watched from lawn, windows, and porch roofs, as the long line of delegates in brilliant academic robes marched around Rockefeller Hall between a double line of undergraduates, the seniors in cap and gown, the underclassmen in white dresses.

The ceremonies themselves were impressive. As the guests assembled the Goldman Band played several selections, including "Building of America" by Goldman, the Tannhäuser Overture, "Pomp and Circumstance" by Elgar, and "University" by Goldman.

The invocation was given by Dr. Rufus M. Jones.

INVOCATION

Let us pray. Eternal and ever loving Father, as we pass over the invincible line which separates the century that is passed from the century yet to venture on, we pause in reverent thanksgiving. The foundations of this College were laid in faith and prayer. For a hundred years it has been dedicated to truth and light and service.

Today with devout hearts we thank Thee for its beneficent life and mission, for its daughters who are now an influence for good in every land in the world, for its noble teachers who have inspired and guided them, for the devoted woman who has built her life into the visible and the invisible college as an inherent part of its structure like a pillar in the temple, to go no more out forever.

We pray Thy benediction may rest upon this College and Thy presence hallow it as a home of truth through all the years that are to come. We ask in Christ's name. Amen.

The congregation then sang a hymn traditional at Mount Holyoke commencements, "O God, our help in ages past."

PRESIDENT WOOLLEY: When the rigors of winter were past, we looked forward to welcoming you all as our guests. Possibly you think that whereas we have met with general co-operation within and without the College, there is a single exception, notably, the Clerk of the Weather. But we hope that the inside will seem so bright that you will forget that the sun is not shining upon us.

Two hundred years before Mount Holyoke opened its doors, exactly two hundred years before the granting of the charter to Mount Holyoke in 1836, there was started within the new country a college destined to become one of the greatest institutions of learning in the world.

It is an honor to have our program opened with greetings from Harvard University. I cannot refrain from adding that Mount Holyoke has a personal interest in the first speaker of the morning, since his mother was a Mount Holyoke graduate in the Class of 1865. Perhaps from her as well as from his father he learned the lesson of statesmanship and wise counsel. It is my pleasure to introduce to this audience Mr. Jerome Davis Greene, Secretary to the Corporation of Harvard University.

GREETINGS FROM THE OLDEST
AMERICAN UNIVERSITY

JEROME DAVIS GREENE

Secretary to the Corporation of Harvard University

The College of John Harvard salutes the College of Mary Lyon on its hundredth birthday. An institution which pointed the way to the higher education of women has a special right to the veneration which age inspires; for it can claim not only priority in age but also the honor reserved for the makers of a great tradition. A true seminary it was, not only in the sense which the era of its foundation frequently applied to all institutions of learning, but also as a *seed plot* where the ideals and hopes and labors of a devoted founder took root and flowered in the College of today, disseminating their fruitage in the lives of thousands of your daughters; flowered, too, in scores of other colleges which can trace their inspiration to the faith and daring of Mary Lyon. Like Sir Walter Mildmay, founder of John Harvard's College of Emmanuel, she might have said, "I have set an Acorn, which when it becomes an Oak, God alone knows what will be the fruit thereof."

God alone knew; for the founder of Mount Holyoke could not have dreamt of the great number and diversity of careers that the coming century would open to women—careers for which higher education would be a prerequisite. To say this is not quite to say that she built more wisely than she knew; for if teaching then seemed likely to be preëminently the career for educated women, she saw further than other leaders of her time into the future of that profession. Moreover, in so doing, she did not narrow her conception of the purpose of liberal education. No false antithesis between training for a profession and training for life was in her mind. It was in order that women as such, women as members of the community, women as builders and protectors of family life, should be equal to the highest intellectual and spiritual demands of these relationships and responsibilities, and equipped for the fullest realization of their individual capacities, that Mary Lyon labored with indomitable courage and patience to establish this College. When, with the social and economic changes the century was soon to bring, the opportunities and privileges of women were enlarged, no new principle had to be invoked to justify the opening to them of all the resources of liberal education. The demand for it was vastly multiplied, but the reason for it had been laid down when Mount Holyoke was founded.

It is a happy circumstance that the Centennial of one of the first institutions for the higher education of women in the United States so nearly coincides with the third centennial of collegiate education in this country. For it unites us all at this time in reverence to the faith and zeal of the founders and in the re-dedication of all colleges and universities to their high and indispensable function in our American democracy. Never has it been more essential that the lamp of learning should be fed, and that its light should be held aloft, than in these troubled times.

Of the light here lit by your sainted founder and zealously tended by her successors it may be said, in the words of Governor Bradford, " . . . as one small candle may light a thousand, so the light here kindled hath shone to many, yea in some sort to our whole nation; let the glorious name of Jehova have all the praise!"

We beg you to accept the hearty congratulations of Harvard University upon the completion of your first century and our fervent hopes for your happiness and prosperity in the century to come.

PRESIDENT WOOLLEY: Yesterday, the day dedicated to the alumnae of Mount Holyoke, there was emphasis upon the international as well as the national work of Mary Lyon. It is fitting that we should have on our platform this morning not only representatives of this country, but also representatives of the lands across the sea, and especially of the land to which we are bound by so many and such enduring ties.

We are fortunate in having as the speaker who brings to us a message from the United Kingdom, a woman who entered into the tradition of public service by her birth; who has worked along many lines of service in her own country; who was the one woman representing the United Kingdom at the Geneva Conference on the Reduction and Limitation of Armaments.

With personal as well as official pleasure I present to you as our next speaker Mrs. Margery Corbett Ashby, who will speak to us on Women in Public Affairs.

WOMEN IN PUBLIC AFFAIRS

Margery Corbett Ashby

President of the International Alliance of Women

Madame President: I wish I were more capable of expressing in words my affection and admiration for yourself, and my gratitude for your services. I am the more diffident in facing such an audience when I remember acutely my first speech in the United States of America at St. Louis. I had done my best, but before any polite applause could be given, the small daughter of my hostess cried out "What queer talk comes out of Mrs. Ashby's mouth!" For that talk and that accent I must ask your indulgence today.

Yesterday as I saw the affectionate greeting given to Dr. Mary Woolley in this great hall I reflected with pride that I could fill such a hall in her honour in thirty-six different countries. Women of thirty-six countries would flock to pay her tribute, and this for two reasons: firstly, because her work for peace and good understanding between peoples at Geneva has brought her into contact with women of all nations; but secondly, because she is the symbol of a great nation which is proud to acknowledge the capacity of its women for service, is proud to give them opportunities for leadership. In a world threatened by the reaction of dictatorship, our eyes turn with hope and trust to this great democracy.

Mary Lyon stood at the beginning of the great movement that brought what is called emancipation for women. The workers were few, but they had the enthusiasm and keenness that goes with a new idea. Those women realized, as we do now, that marriage involves a greater change of occupation for women than for men, so that women have not only to be educated for a known profession or work, but also prepared for the unknown demands on their intelligence which family life may bring. Women were therefore more, not less, in need of education than men, and an education which could give not only information, but also a power of initiative, a sense of responsibility, and a capacity to adapt themselves to varying situations.

It has been said that men deal in wealth and women in loves. To some extent this is true, which adds yet another reason for the education of women. Woman's brain must be sufficiently developed to comprehend standards of hygiene and morality, and to realize her social responsibility. Only those who wrestle to improve social conditions in India and the Near East can understand the appalling handicap it is to a community if there are no women educated so that they can give it service as teachers, doctors, nurses, voluntary and paid social workers. It is such women who set the standard of marriage.

In the old days a woman's only prospect was to "marry for a home," and this obscured the highest aspect of marriage, the spiritual partnership. If, however, there is a possibility of a happy, full life other than marriage, it is possible once more to give marriage its true significance.

Women are now educated in most countries, but opportunities for responsibility and leadership, though they are increasing, are still few. It is to gain these opportunities that is the new aim of the Women's Movement.

How many women are government executives? How many are heads of great educational establishments? How many are heads of big industrial concerns? Are women less capable than men when given the chance?

In British history women have seen new needs before men. It was Elizabeth Fry who first began to agitate for reform of the prisons. Florence Nightingale showed the way for hospitals and trained nurses. Josephine Butler first saw the injustice and inconsistency of State profit from vice and a double standard of morality, and it was she who had the energy and persistence to get both abolished.

Bertha von Suttner, the Austrian, in her famous book *Lay Down Your Arms* was the founder of the present peace movement, with its reverence for justice and law, and its horror of war and imperialism. The forerunner of Jane Addams, Amalie Sieveking of Germany, laid the foundations of social work.

Our right to earn our living and to be full citizens of our country we owe to the pioneer women—Louise Otto Peters of Germany, Dame Millicent Fawcett of England, Dr. Aletta Jacob of Holland, and, nearer our own day, to Mrs. Chapman Catt, Mrs. Pankhurst, the Duchess of Atholl, Madame Brunschwicq, Madame Malaterre-Sellier, Miss Gertrude Bell, Madame Palencia, Madame Kolontai, Mlle Renson, Mrs. Bakker Nort, Mlle Kluyver, Madame Mundt.

All these women won their goal, acquired their leadership by sheer force of character against contempt, ridicule, slander and physical violence, of a bitterness we can hardly realize today.

The opposition is still here, but it is disguised. Any one of us, however timid and soft, can be educated; the lower ranks of employment at lower rates of pay are open to us; there is social and personal freedom, *but* this has its disadvantages. Because school and college are easy, because the young girl is welcomed for her cheapness in office, factory, and workshop, we believe we have equality and freedom, and can gain the goal of leadership or wealth equally with men. This is a delusion; we generally discover after ten years of work that we are passed over for promotion, and that the difference between men's and women's salaries and opportunities yawns more widely. We still need the loyalty and comradeship among women that won us the world of today. We must break the vicious circle which denies us posts of leadership and responsibility, because we have not had the experience which society has denied us.

Yet the world today is full of examples of outstanding women who have been given, or who have seized their chance. Today not only national but international service is open to us. World service for women was opened when the women of America and of the Allied Powers secured the insertion in the Covenant of the League of Nations of the third clause of Article 7.

All positions under and in connection with the League, including the Secretariat, shall be open equally to men and women.

Miss Wilson of the United States of America created the first library of the League with the magnificent Rockefeller Foundation she secured for it. Her contract was not renewed when her work was showy enough for a man to want it.

Dame Rachel Crowdy built up the humanitarian and social side of the League, organized the world fight against the traffic in opium and dangerous drugs, against the traffic for immoral purposes of women and children, and the struggle for higher standards of child care and protection. Jockeyed out of a permanent contract, she was replaced by two men, one at the higher grade salary she had been refused, when she was shouldering the whole responsibility.

Dr. Janet Campbell was lent by the British Government to the League to set up a new world standard for the protection of child life and maternity.

Dame Adelaide Anderson, retiring as chief woman factory inspector and about to enjoy a lazy and happy world tour, was summoned by cable by the Chinese Government to help them eliminate child workers from their factories.

One of the most important articles in the Covenant of the League is Article 22, wherein State Members of the League accept the principle of trusteeship in mandated territories. Women's organizations fought for and obtained the provision that a woman should be a member of the Mandates Commission, since guardianship of a race implies guardianship of the family and social life. Mrs. Brigge Wicksel, Swedish international lawyer of repute, set a magnificent standard of work. Small, bright-eyed, mouse-like, she faced and won over, by knowledge and character, the most impressive administrators of the great colonial empires—Belgium, Great Britain, France, Holland, Spain, and Portugal. She is succeeded by Miss Dannevieg of Norway, equally fine champion of the weak.

The Commission that fights prostitution and encourages child welfare is largely composed of women representatives of governments. Among these remarkable women we find Countess Apponyi of Hungary, Miss Forchhammer of Denmark, Madame Woniatowski the labor expert and Madame Szelagowska the social expert, both of Poland.

The countries that freed themselves from the ancient empires of Russia and Austria and the new empire of Germany have produced remarkable women. They have had their chance because their men folk recognized that they needed all the good will and intelligence the community could produce to build the new state firmly and securely.

Czechoslovakia has produced Senator Plaminkova, who defends the national budget in the Senate, and works indefatigably for peace, for national prosperity, and for women. When Parliament proposed to replace the women heads of women's educational establishments by men, Plaminkova, with the women behind her, smashingly defeated such a ridiculous proposal.

Denmark and Great Britian have had women Ministers for Education. Even France, that denies women the vote, has two women Under-Secretaries of State, Madame Brunschwicq and

Mlle Lacore, who deal with all aspects of education and child welfare.

Women in the East have rendered even more remarkable service. Madame Charaoui Pasha, after attending the Alliance Conference in Rome in 1923, threw aside her veil and dedicated her intelligence, her social standing and wealth to gaining independence for Egyptian women, founding schools, technical colleges, orphanages, and reviving the ancient pottery of Egypt. Mlle Ceza Nabaraoui, the talented editor of *L'Egyptienne*, was the first woman Moslem lawyer. She challenged in the law courts the degradation of women's rights which had been imposed for centuries on Mohammed's original conception.

India is grateful to many remarkable women. Sarojini Naidhu, poetess and passionate nationalist, Dr. Muthulaksmi Reddi, Chairman of the Bombay Municipal Council, ardent social workers. Mrs. Sen, the enthusiastic and devoted head of the Lady Irwin College for Women, which unites, for a particularly modern and effective education, girls of each of India's many races and creeds, a constructive example of enormous value to that communally obsessed country. Raja Kumari Amrit Kaur, through the long deliberations on the new constitution, defended women's interests with the coolest courage and devotion.

In Japan women suffer as the men do from the temporary success of the militarist party, but Mrs. Gauntlett has for years led the movement for suffrage, for temperance, and for peace, with dignity and immense courage.

Unfortunately I know less well the women of South America, but Dr. Paulina Luisi often represented the Government of Uruguay at medical conferences and at Geneva, and Bertha Lutz, M. P., is the ardent champion of women's rights in Brazil.

In Africa Madame Mazorati of Belgium developed a system of welfare work and home industries for the native races better than any Great Britain or France can claim to have done. She has proved herself a dauntless champion of the home, of women and of children, as the one woman on the Commission on Forced Labour under the International Labour Office.

I could continue endlessly the tale of women's service, but the moral is more important. Women have given, can give, precious service to the world, but the world must pay the price, if it is to benefit. The price is first education, then opportunity. Loyalty of women to women, fair play from men.

Women must be inspired by a deep faith in democracy, a passionate belief in freedom, in their own value, and have a resolute determination that what former generations have won, they will not throw away. The menace of Fascism lies dark over Europe. Are you free from it? Are your horizons expanding, or do you see insidiously creeping in an attack on women's opportunities and chances? The price of freedom is eternal vigilance.

I come from Europe, where democracy is slowly being throttled, and Christianity is denied. Education is denied to young women, avenues closed, and women have been thrown out of positions just because they are women, even where they had built up new social services. Even in my beloved country, in the last four years we have sacrificed our civil liberty where our fathers and mothers would have risen in its defence. Speaking for all women who are near the dark shadow of tyranny and despotism, I say to you not "Come over and help us," but instead "Be true to your own selves and thus help us." Unless you can make democracy a successful coefficient in the United States it cannot survive elsewhere. We need your help on lines in which this great College is a pioneer. It stands for the full development of personality, for tolerance, for Christian faith, for reverence for truth without regard to prejudice of race and sex. How can we rise above this flood of obscurantism that is sweeping over Europe, where free speech hardly exists any more, where prisons are over full of men and women whose only crime is their faith in liberty and free speech? This is the moment when, if women wish to make a contribution to the solution of world problems, they must above all have faith in themselves. Democracy cannot perish from attack from without, but only if it is betrayed from within.

PRESIDENT WOOLLEY: My memory goes back so far that I can recall statements that women, if given added opportunities, would not show solidarity, unity. It is so common an experience to have women working together, as for example, in the League of Women Voters, the American Association of University Women, the Federation of Women's Clubs, that we have almost forgotten that there was once a disbelief in women's ability to do this very thing.

Our next speaker is a woman who has done much to further the cause of unity among college women in this country through the American Association of University Women, through the League of Women Voters, and in other ways. Toward the close of the War she was one of the founders of the International Federation of University Women, and for the second time, is the President of that Federation.

It gives me pleasure to introduce a great civic servant in our foremost city, as well as a great internationalist, Virginia Crocheron Gildersleeve, Dean of Barnard College and the President of the International Federation of University Women.

THE BRIGHT COUNTENANCE OF TRUTH

VIRGINIA CROCHERON GILDERSLEEVE

President of the International Federation of University Women and Dean of Barnard College

Women in Scholarly Pursuits is the subject on which I was asked to speak at this memorable celebration, in contrast with the discussion of women in public affairs which we have heard from the previous speaker. They make a good pair of topics, for unless some people engage in scholarly pursuits, those who grapple with public affairs will not be armed to deal with them wisely and effectively.

It is fitting, moreover, that we should meditate for a time on scholarly pursuits at this commemoration of a hundred years of honest labor in the training of young students in the foundations of scholarship.

To some few human beings scholarly pursuits—the scholar's life and work—seem a privilege and a joy. This life was beautifully described long ago by John Milton, who, forced by his conscience into public affairs, looked back regretfully on the privilege of "beholding the bright countenance of truth in the quiet and still air of delightful studies." I know no better words to hold up as my banner and my text.

"Beholding the bright countenance of truth." To the humble toiler at the foundations, as well as to the great creative scholar, comes at times the consciousness of seeing new truth. This sense of pushing out into the darkness that surrounds mankind the bright boundary of knowledge, of lifting the veil from mysteries, of gazing on the Grail, is one of the great spiritual experiences possible to man.

"The quiet and still air of delightful studies." The scholar's life is indeed a refuge from the tumult and the shouting, from the conflicts of a troubled world, and from the unrest and the anguish of personal human emotions. It is right that he should be sheltered. The mediaeval monastery, the lamasery of Shangri-La in *Lost Horizon*—we shall always need some "ivory towers" such as these, to provide that quiet and still air in which the scholars can live and work.

Milton's lovely words, on which I have been embroidering, portray a way of life intensely attractive to some human beings. But from the privilege of beholding the bright countenance of truth in the quiet and still air of delightful studies one part of mankind, women, have been generally shut out during most of the history of our race.

At times, however, in the more remote past, and most especially in recent years, women have been admitted to these pursuits. During the hundred years since Mount Holyoke opened, have women's scholarly opportunities increased? Immensely so: there is no doubt about that. This century has seen most universities opened to women, women's colleges established, fellowships for advanced work such as those of the Guggenheim Foundation and the National Research Council made available for qualified women, and positions in the great research institutes opened to them, not only the posts as junior helpers but the important research positions.

With these opportunities available, many women have tasted of the joys of scholarly pursuits; a fair number have achieved considerable results; and a few have contributed notably to the sum total of human knowledge. Let us recognize this advance today, and give thanks.

It is not my purpose to rehearse the detailed history of this great movement, nor to name the individual women who have achieved scholarly distinction. I wish rather to attempt to estimate our present position in this spring of 1937, and reflect on some circumstances which affect the life of the woman scholar today.

In this field, as in almost all others, women workers have of course been put back and cut off by the economic exigencies of the great depression, and by the political and social philosophies of the foreign dictatorships. In this country their chances have been affected considerably by the first influence and somewhat by the second. On the whole, however, most thinking people in this republic now admit,—or should I say *still* admit?—that women are human beings with many of the mental characteristics of other human beings.

Those of you who have read Margaret Mead's somewhat startling book, *Sex and Temperament*, may agree that the sexes are far less different from each other than most people believe. Are they different on the scholarly side, or identical? After a lifetime spent in a great university of both sexes, I conjecture that for perhaps nine-tenths of their intellectual qualities and four-fifths of their emotional qualities male and female human beings are in general identical. Individuals, of course, vary very widely.

In the range of the identical qualities of the two sexes lie, I believe, the scholarly tastes and abilities. Few women possess them; and few men.

The identical nature of the intellectual qualities of the two sexes is somewhat obscured by the physical differences between them, and most of all by the great differences in the *circumstances* of the lives of most individual men and women, brought about largely by this physical variance.

If, so far as intellect is concerned, we are as likely—or nearly as likely—to find a scholar among women as among men, then, unless we can change or mitigate the circumstances of life which may bar her from intellectual fruition, we may be losing for the human race a Pasteur or a Plato.

This has been more and more realized during the last half century and we have made considerable progress in mitigating the circumstances of feminine life and the background of public opinion which have barred women from scholarly pursuits. Just how does the situation stand at this moment?

In one way scholarly pursuits are less attractive to women now than they were fifty or even twenty-five years ago. Young women scholars no longer feel the zest of pioneers and crusaders. To be told that you are incapable of doing a thing is a great incentive to doing it! The desire to demonstrate that your sex has as much brains as Brother John's is a real stimulus. Being taken now more as a matter of course, women scholars lack these incentives.

Partly for this reason, perhaps, fewer women today desire to lead a celibate life and sacrifice the human relationships of marriage and motherhood on the altar of scholarship. At the present moment the great majority of young scholars, male and female, want to marry and have children. There is no use blinking the fact that for the women this means some interruption in their scholarly pursuits.

Some types of scholarly work, it is true, blend rather well with family life, since they may be adjusted to hours and seasons and to family emergencies; but others present difficulties. Moreover, in the scholarly world of America research must often be combined with college or university teaching, and this causes complications. In my own college we allow the married women on our staff leave of absence with pay for childbearing and we are watching with interest this experiment in adjusting the new pattern of life for women.

Even without a husband and a family the woman scholar is today still somewhat handicapped as compared with the man. In that remarkable book *A Room of One's Own* Virginia Woolf has vividly portrayed the material and social obstacles clogging the advance of the intellectual worker of the female sex. Do you remember her moving account of Shakespeare's sister Judith, as gifted as her brother, a "poet's heart caught and tangled in a woman's body"?

Such material and social obstacles are vastly less, at this moment in this country, than they were for the general run of women in England in the sixteenth century; but they have not disappeared. As Virginia Woolf says, "a woman must have money and a room of her own if she is to write fiction." So must she if she is to be a scholar. And money and a room of one's own are still a little harder for a woman to achieve than for a man.

It is not only that Johnnie and Jennie and the cook are more likely to enter the door of mother's study than to invade father's; even the celibate woman scholar is still more likely than the man to have to care for an aged parent or a foolish nephew. We are generally not so good at evading family claims.

In colleges and universities also our rooms are not quite so fully our own. For one reason or another women professors are more likely to be cluttered up with students' personal problems and with committee and social responsibilities than are men. We must resist this tendency, we of the administration and the faculty, and hang the "Busy: Keep Out" sign on the doors of our most promising women scholars, so as not to violate the quiet and still air of the rooms that should be their own.

A room of one's own—*and money*, says Mrs. Woolf. Is it as easy for a woman scholar to get the money? So far as I am aware, the various research councils and fellowship foundations are ready to consider fairly and with open mind applications from women and to deal with them on their scholarly merits. It is less easy for our sex to gain those professorships in colleges and universities which are so often the necessary ivory towers for the pursuing of delightful studies. True, we have made great progress in the last hundred years in opening professorships to women but not much, I imagine, in the last twenty-five, for we have not many more women professors in coeducational universities, and we have proportionately fewer in women's colleges.

As for the coeducational institutions, I have never been familiar with them, and so I hazard only very tentatively the conjecture that in them women are still regarded definitely as an inferior sex. The impression I gather from my casual and enjoyable visits at coeducational universities is that women stay in their place. No one seems to expect a woman to become the head of the institution or the dean of a faculty, and only rarely a professor of full standing; and no one conceives of a woman student as president of the student body, or editor-in-chief of the university paper, or holding any other post of chief responsibility. Men are quite naturally expected to do the leading. This atmosphere of expected subservience on the part of our sex—in which I must say they seem for the most part quite happy—strikes oddly the visitor from a college for women, who feels, perhaps wrongly, that it may tend to keep women from those professorial niches in which human beings can so delightfully pursue the scholarly life.

Not faring very well professorially in coeducational institutions, in colleges for women, oddly enough, they have fared less well in recent years than before, just because women are more open-minded and impartial on this question, apparently, than men. Women's colleges realize that it is well for young people to be taught by both men and women: that no scholarly or academic community should consist of one sex only. So of recent years even those colleges for women whose faculties used to consist almost entirely of women have made a distinct effort to secure a considerable proportion of men professors. This is a sound policy; I applaud it. It tends to make a more live and varied, a less cloistered community on the campus.

But in this situation our sex seems to be losing out on both fronts. Unless we can persuade our colleagues in the colleges for men to take a view as broad-minded as our own, and realize that they should have a fair proportion of women teaching their boys, our women scholars, alas, will find very few professorial posts available to provide money and a room of their own for the pursuit of the scholarly life.

This is not so impossible, I believe, as it may sound. I think I see a few faint signs that some day, conceivably, posts in men's colleges may be available for women scholars.

Looking back over the century that has passed, the dominant emotion of the woman scholar today must be one of thankfulness that such immense progress has been made in opening to human beings of the female sex the doors that lead to delightful studies and to the vision of the bright countenance of truth. We can feel confident that, in spite of temporary setbacks, we shall go on advancing in the sympathetic understanding and adjustment of the problems of a scholar's life. Shakespeare's sister—to recur to Virginia Woolf's parable—will not need to be driven to a suicide's grave at the crossroads.

Here in this beautiful valley in the New England hills, at all events, Mount Holyoke College will continue to open to her daughters not only the pathways to active service in world affairs, to a good fight for the right, and to happy and useful lives in home and community, but also the quiet doors that lead to the scholar's never ending search for truth.

PRESIDENT WOOLLEY: The Federal Government of the United States pays us the honor of sending a representative of its Department of State to be our guest and speaker.

Throughout the years, the citizens of the United States have had reason to be proud of the Department of State. I think we have never had a Department which has worked more unitedly and with greater ability at the tremendous problem facing the nations, that of learning how to live together.

I am glad to welcome in behalf of the College, Francis Bowes Sayre, Assistant Secretary of State of the United States, who will speak to us on Woman and Peace.

WOMAN AND PEACE

FRANCIS BOWES SAYRE

Assistant Secretary of State

It is a joy to take part in an observance such as the present one. We are here to commemorate the one hundredth anniversary of an institution which for this long span has been a continuing constructive influence in the life of our country. A pioneer in education for women, Mount Holyoke College has, with each graduating class, added to the growing proportion of our people who are equipped to take a more intelligent and more informed part in public affairs. Under the guidance of succeeding presidents and teachers—able and sincerely devoted to the great ideals for which this institution was founded— Mount Holyoke has stimulated and inspired generation after generation of American womanhood to make American life richer and more rewarding. An institution such as this could not fail to make a mark upon the life of America—never more so, indeed, than since the turn of the century under the brilliant leadership of Mount Holyoke's distinguished president, Dr. Mary Emma Woolley.

Dr. Woolley is a commanding figure in the field of education. Within this field she has rendered notable and distinguished service. Yet she has done far more. Her spirit has been too large, her devotion to public affairs too fervent to be confined altogether within the realm of education. Within educational fields she could guide, enlighten, inspire. But her tireless spirit compelled her to go beyond this and to take an active and practical part in some of the greatest issues of the day, particularly in seeking to promote better relations among the nations of the world. As a member of many societies working for peace and better international understanding, she has made an invaluable contribution to this vital phase of our national life. The Government of the United States recognized her preëminence in this field by appointing her a member of the American Delegation to the World Conference for the Reduction and Limitation of Armaments.

Dr. Woolley's interests and activities are symbolical of the rôle which intelligent and educated women can and should play in the public affairs of our country. There is no domain of life in which qualities of understanding and leadership are more desperately needed today than in that of international relationships. For upon the character of these relations depends the greatest issue with which humanity is confronted today—the issue of war and peace. And upon that issue may well depend the future existence or tragic shipwreck of our whole civilization.

More than eighteen years have passed since guns were stilled at the conclusion of the greatest war in the world's history. At that time there was a universal and burning desire to end war and to build for peace. Yet war has not been ended. Since those poignant days of 1918, the flames of war have broken out and seared more than one portion of the globe. And today, in an atmosphere of almost unprecedented tension, millions of people everywhere live in fear of the possibility of a new and even greater catastrophe than that which shattered the peace of the world in 1914.

During these years, military technology has made enormous strides. The grim drama of the Spanish civil war is a terrifying revelation of what modern warfare means in unutterable suffering and destruction. But the supreme tragedy of war lies not in lost lives and shattered bodies. It lies rather in the folly and utter futility of the sacrifice. For war solves no problems. It merely multiplies them. And it multiplies, too, years of intense suffering caused by the economic and social dislocations which inevitably follow in its wake. Indeed, even more than the actual clash of arms, these ensuing dislocations undermine all constructive activity and render war a deadly peril to our civilization itself.

Fortunately, side by side with the increased deadliness of implements of war, have come increased efforts to prevent war, based upon intelligent study and understanding of its underlying causes. We are beginning to realize more and more clearly that modern war is largely the result of economic factors and of uncoöperative commercial policies which tend to kill international trade.

One of the fundamental and inescapable facts of today is the utter economic interdependence of the world. No great industrial nation is or can possibly be economically independent. To achieve economic self-sufficiency would be to set the clock back more than one hundred years, to eliminate through suffering and slow starvation a substantial part of the people of the world.

Even the United States, probably more nearly self-sufficient than any other great nation, could not by any possibility maintain its present standard of living on the basis of self-sufficiency. We need rubber for our automobile tires, tin for our containers, antimony for our telephone equipment, jute for our burlap bags, hemp for our rope. We require large quantities of silk, tea chocolate, bananas and other tropical products which we cannot grow. Our industries require foreign nickel, manganese, tungsten, newsprint, wood pulp and a long list of goods not produced here in sufficient quantity.

If our standard of living and our prosperity are dependent upon imports, they are no less vitally dependent upon exports. We are utterly dependent on foreign markets. Our national economy has been geared to support millions of workers in occupations which have come to be vitally dependent on foreign markets. Strip those industries of their foreign market and you drive millions of Americans out of the only forms of employment by which many of them can live and seriously affect the prosperity of millions of other Americans through the curtailment of domestic markets.

Lowered standards of living, as a result of economic isolation, would cause intense suffering and acute social disorders in the United States; in Europe, where nations lack the rich diversity of resources which we enjoy, thorough-going economic isolation would entail in many countries actual starvation.

Once the stubborn reality of the vital interdependence of nations is clearly realized, the nature of the foundations required for a stable peace becomes clear. Today the standards of living, if not the very lives, of entire populations are dependent upon a steady inflow of raw materials and foodstuffs at prices unenhanced by prohibitive economic barriers, and also upon a steady sale of their own surplus production in foreign markets for a remunerative return.

Men will fight before they starve. They may also fight rather than see accustomed standards of living reduced to unbearable levels.

There can be no real security for any nation, industrial or agricultural, and consequently there can be no lasting international peace or stability, until nations can secure for themselves access, free from prohibitive nationalistic barriers, first to necessary raw materials and foodstuffs, and second to foreign markets.

Peace will not come through mere desire. Peace will come only as we build for it firm and sound foundations in our national commercial policies and in our political life. That means the cultivation of economic relations among nations which make for friendliness, fairness and mutual advantage.

Whatever policies militate against peace cannot be American. America must stand firmly against a policy of economic nationalism. Americans cannot forget that the strength of the nation from the very outset was built upon the frank recognition of the interdependence of the sovereign American States. Our Constitution expressly forbade the creation of trade barriers or customs tariffs against goods from other states. It is this, perhaps as largely as any other provision in the Constitution, that has given strength to the nation, stability and peace to the States. Practical experience has proved the worth of this, the American way.

By her trade-agreements program America has already taken a significant and an important step in this direction. Thus far the program has been more than justified by the practical results of the agreements already entered into, as evidenced by marked increases in foreign trade and by their influence in encouraging a world-wide reëxamination of the means of freeing international trade from its nationalistic fetters.

In building for peace, our Government needs the support of all public-spirited citizens. And it is to the graduates of institutions like Mount Holyoke that we must look for leaders and inspirers of informed public opinion by which alone, in the final analysis, national policies are shaped.

This is the message which, as the representative of the United States Government, I bring to you. Our country is fortunate beyond measure in having, at this critical juncture in world affairs, a President and a Secretary of State who are sincerely and whole-heartedly devoted to the cause of peace. But they can succeed only as the men and women of our entire nation dedicate themselves with fervor and understanding to the support of those policies upon which alone can rest a durable peace.

CONFERRING OF HONORARY DEGREES

After the singing of "America" by the audience occurred the presentation of candidates for honorary degrees, by Dr. A. Elizabeth Adams, Professor of Zoology and Chief Marshal of the occasion. The introductions and the citations by President Woolley follow:

DOCTOR OF LETTERS

DOROTHY CANFIELD FISHER. Graduate of Ohio State University, a doctor of Columbia University, both in course and by honorary degree; serving in humanitarian work in France during three years of the World War; writer of articles and books translated into many tongues.

Dorothy Canfield Fisher, distinguished daughter of a distinguished father, claimed by other peoples through the wide translations of your stories; using your literary gift for the furtherance of many a good cause; ardent champion of international understanding; in the name of the Board of Trustees of Mount Holyoke College, I confer upon you the honorary degree of Doctor of Letters and admit you to all its rights and privileges.

FRANCES LESTER WARNER HERSEY. Graduate of Mount Holyoke, instructor at Mount Holyoke and at Wellesley Colleges, Assistant to the Editor of the *Atlantic Monthly;* author of *Endicott and I* and other essays.

Frances Lester Warner Hersey, devoted daughter of Mount Holyoke, gifted essayist, adding to your power of insight and of literary expression a whimsical gift of the gods, as rare as it is precious; in the name of the Trustees of Mount Holyoke College, I confer upon you the honorary degree of Doctor of Letters and admit you to all its rights and privileges.

MALVINA HOFFMAN. Sculptor, member of the Scientific Staff of the Field Museum of Chicago, pupil of Gutzon Borglum and Auguste

SENIORS READY TO DECORATE THE FOUNDER'S GRAVE

ALUMNAE RECIPIENTS OF HONORARY DEGREES
Left to right: Mary Ely Lyman, Margaret Tyler, Yau Tsit Law
Emily Susan Wilson, Frances Warner Hersey

Rodin, holder of many prizes in this country and in Europe, permanent exhibitor in leading art museums and galleries of the world.

Malvina Hoffman, scientist and artist to whom all women owe a debt of gratitude, not only for your artistic achievement, but also for your idealism, your high standard of attainment, your human sympathy and spiritual insight which have made you an interpreter as well as a great artist; in the name of the Trustees of Mount Holyoke College, I confer upon you the honorary degree Doctor of Letters, and admit you to all its rights and privileges.

YAU TSIT LAW. Graduate of Mount Holyoke; connected for many years with True Light Seminary and School of Canton, China; at one time Dean of Women at Lingnan University in Canton and with the Young Women's Christian Association of Southern China; member of the China Commission on Christian education in 1921, and of the Institute of Pacific Affairs in Honolulu in 1927.

Yau Tsit Law, representative of Mount Holyoke's daughters in the Far East; for twenty years serving your country and countrywomen as educator and Christian worker; representing your people on two important International Commissions and Conferences; in the name of the Trustees of Mount Holyoke College, I confer upon you the honorary degree of Doctor of Letters and admit you to all its rights and privileges.

EVA LE GALLIENNE. Founder and Director of the Civic Repertory Theatre of New York.

Eva Le Gallienne, born in England, educated in France, proudly claimed by the United States as her own, recipient of many honors in recognition of your contribution, not only to dramatic art, but also to the social and political life of our day; in the name of the Trustees of Mount Holyoke College, I confer upon you the honorary degree of Doctor of Letters and admit you to all its rights and privileges.

MARY REDINGTON ELY LYMAN. Graduate of Mount Holyoke, Bachelor of Sacred Theology of Union Theological Seminary, Fellow of Union Seminary at the University of Cambridge; Doctor of the University of Chicago, now Lecturer in the English Bible at Union Seminary and Associate in Religion at Barnard College.

Mary Redington Ely Lyman, outstanding scholar in the writings of the New Testament, possessor of a three-fold gift—the ability of the research worker, the teacher and the writer; a daughter whom Mount Holyoke delights to honor; in the name of the Trustees of Mount Holyoke College, I confer upon you the honorary degree of Doctor of Letters, and admit you to all its rights and privileges.

Eileen Power. Student at Girton College and of the Sorbonne; Shaw Research Student at the London School of Economics and Political Science; Director of Studies in History at Girton College, now Professor of Economic History in the London School of Economics.

Eileen Power, scholar and writer; holding a post of honor in one of the foremost schools of the world; an illustrious example of what women are accomplishing in the field of scholarship; in the name of the Trustees of Mount Holyoke College, I confer upon you the honorary degree of Doctor of Letters and admit you to all its rights and privileges.

Alice Ravenel Huger Smith. Outstanding water-colorist, joint writer with her father of the one authoritative book on Charleston's old houses, author of many articles, especially on miniature painting and painters.

Alice Ravenel Huger Smith, talented daughter of the South, enriching our national life by your gifts as artist and writer; in the name of the Trustees of Mount Holyoke College, I confer upon you the honorary degree of Doctor of Letters and admit you to all its rights and privileges.

Léonie Villard. Doctor of the University of Paris; Professor of English and American Literature at the University of Lyons, Honorary President of the Lyons Branch of the International Federation of University Women, Visiting Carnegie Professor in the United States.

Léonie Villard, first woman in France to hold a chair of literature in a French university; writer of distinction in the English literary and in the American dramatic field, as well as on the life of your own people, welcomed at Mount Holyoke as Visiting Professor whom we wish also to claim as one of our daughters; in the name of the Trustees of Mount Holyoke College, I confer upon you the honorary degree of Doctor of Letters and admit you to all its rights and privileges.

EMILY SUSAN WILSON. Graduate of Mount Holyoke Seminary in 1861; the succeeding two years teacher of Latin and Mathematics at Mount Holyoke; for eighteen years teacher of History at Mills College.

Emily Susan Wilson, according to the records receiving your diploma from Mount Holyoke the year of the beginning of our Civil War, you shake our faith in the veracity of figures! The only way in which we can reconcile you and your statement that it is seventy-six years since you graduated, is by the inference that in your career as a globe-trotter—to Hawaii, the South Seas, and many countries in Europe—you drank deep at numerous fountains of youth; in the name of the Trustees of Mount Holyoke College, I confer upon you the honorary degree of Doctor of Letters and admit you to all its rights and privileges.

ROBERTA TEALE SWARTZ CHALMERS. Graduate of Mount Holyoke, receiving her Master's degree from Radcliffe College, her Bachelor of Letters from Oxford University; for five years on the staff of the Department of English at Mount Holyoke; now Associate Professor at Rockford College.

Roberta Teale Swartz Chalmers, student and poet, daughter whose career we watch with pride whether it be that of power behind the throne at Rockford, soon to be changed to Kenyon College, or in your own realm of song; in the name of the Trustees of Mount Holyoke College, I confer upon you the honorary degree of Doctor of Letters and admit you to all its rights and privileges.

DOCTOR OF SCIENCE

MARGARET CLAY FERGUSON. Bachelor of Science, Doctor of Philosophy, and Fellow of Cornell University; for twenty-five years head of the Department of Botany, and now Research Professor of Botany, at Wellesley College; author of many scientific papers, and official in many scientific organizations.

Margaret Clay Ferguson, to whom an outstanding Department of Botany among the colleges for women owes a great debt; to whom all men and women interested in the progress of science are equally indebted; in the name of the Trustees of Mount Holyoke College,

I confer upon you the honorary degree of Doctor of Science and admit you to all its rights and privileges.

MARGARET TYLER. Graduate of Mount Holyoke, Doctor of Medicine of Johns Hopkins Medical School, student in Vienna, Hamburg, and Prague, Resident Physician in Obstetrics in the New Haven Hospital; Associate Clinical Professor of Obstetrics and Gynecology in the Yale Medical School.

Margaret Tyler, representing the many daughters of Mount Holyoke who have found in the mission of healing their inspiration for service; in the name of the Trustees of Mount Holyoke College, I confer upon you the honorary degree of Doctor of Science and admit you to all its rights and privileges.

ANNA PELL WHEELER. Graduate of the University of South Dakota, receiving the Master's degree from Radcliffe College, the doctorate from the University of Chicago; student at the University of Göttingen; member of the Mathematics staff at Mount Holyoke from 1911 to 1918; now Chairman of the Department of Mathematics at Bryn Mawr College.

Anna Pell Wheeler, a scholar whose achievements have been recognized in many ways, among them the invitation from the American Mathematical Society to give a series of lectures at their Eleventh Colloquium, the only woman who has been thus honored; a stimulating teacher and able administrator, as Bryn Mawr and Mount Holyoke Colleges can certify; outstanding, "even in these days of brilliant women in science"; in the name of the Trustees of Mount Holyoke College, I confer upon you the honorary degree of Doctor of Science and admit you to all its rights and privileges.

DOCTOR OF LAWS

KATHARINE BLUNT. Graduate of Vassar College, student at the Massachusetts Institute of Technology, receiving her doctorate in chemistry at the University of Chicago; Instructor in Chemistry at Vassar College; Professor in Home Economics at the University of Chicago; during the War serving in the Department of Agriculture as a member of the Food Administration; since 1929 President of the Connecticut College for Women.

Katharine Blunt, chemist, teacher, and administrator; contributing equally to productive scholarship and to the home; with the trained powers of the scientist attacking the problems of administration, and in less than a decade bringing a great college for women to the front rank; in the name of the Trustees of Mount Holyoke College, I confer upon you the honorary degree of Doctor of Laws and admit you to all its rights and privileges.

MILDRED HELEN McAFEE. Graduate of Vassar College, holding a Master's degree from the University of Chicago; Dean of Women at Center College; Secretary of the Vassar Alumnae Association; Dean of Women at Oberlin College; President of Wellesley College.

Mildred Helen McAfee, claimed by more than one college to which Mount Holyoke wishes to add another, thus giving expression— if I may quote—"not only to its admiration" for you, but also "to the relationship of confidence and affection which has always existed between Wellesley and Mount Holyoke"; in the name of the Trustees of Mount Holyoke College, I confer upon you the honorary degree of Doctor of Laws and admit you to all its rights and privileges.

MARGARET SHOVE MORRISS. Graduate of Goucher College; Doctor of Bryn Mawr College, student at the London School of Economics; for twelve years on the staff of Mount Holyoke College in the Department of History and as administrative officer; serving in France with the War Work Council of the Young Women's Christian Association from 1917 to 1919; Dean of Pembroke College in Brown University; President of the American Association of University Women.

Margaret Shove Morriss, although daughter of another college for women, seeming peculiarly to belong to Mount Holyoke; President of the American Association of University Women and therefore claimed by all college women; for what you have accomplished as Dean of Pembroke College during the last fourteen years; in the name of the Trustees of Mount Holyoke College, I confer upon you the honorary degree of Doctor of Laws and admit you to all its rights and privileges.

AURELIA HENRY REINHARDT. Graduate of the University of California; Fellow at Yale University, from which she received her doctorate; Lecturer in English at the University of California; for twenty years President of Mills College; former President of the American Association of University Women.

Aurelia Henry Reinhardt, President of Mount Holyoke's daughter on the Pacific Coast, whose progress the mother college has watched with pride, a progress that under your leadership has been phenomenal, in beauty of buildings, equipment of departments, and academic strength; in the name of the Trustees of Mount Holyoke College, I confer upon you the honorary degree of Doctor of Laws and admit you to all its rights and privileges.

Virginia Crocheron Gildersleeve. Graduate, Master and Doctor of Columbia University; Instructor, Assistant Professor, Professor and Dean of Barnard College; member of the Judicial Council of the State of New York; Vice Chairman of the American National Committee on International Intellectual Co-operation; Trustee of the Institute of International Education; for the second time President of the International Federation of University Women.

Virginia Crocheron Gildersleeve, daughter of our greatest city, to which you have added distinction by your scholarship, your civic service, and your liberality of thought and action; world citizen, leading the university women of the world into that closer cooperation which makes for international understanding and unity; in the name of the Trustees of Mount Holyoke College, I confer upon you the honorary degree of Doctor of Laws and admit you to all its rights and privileges.

Margery Corbett Ashby. Student of Newnham College, where she took the classical Tripos, President of the British Commonwealth League and many other national organizations; since 1923 President of the International Alliance of Women; appointed by the British Government as the only woman on the Delegation of the United Kingdom to the Conference for the Reduction and Limitation of Armaments.

Margery Corbett Ashby, inheritor of a liberal tradition, "in which equality of men and women and service for the public good were taken for granted," adding to your public service in your own country that for international understanding, to which you have brought your linguistic gift, your understanding of other peoples and countries, and your conviction that a new world order must be established on moral as well as physical disarmament; in the name of the Trustees of Mount Holyoke College, I confer upon you the honorary degree of Doctor of Laws and admit you to all its rights and privileges.

Of the twenty distinguished women who were recipients of these honorary degrees, six were graduates of Mount Holyoke. One of them, Roberta Teale Swartz Chalmers, had written the Centennial poem which she now read with such expression and feeling as to win appreciative response.

GAUDEAMUS IGITUR ALSO, MARY LYON!
Centennial Poem

The leaves fall
And the crows cry,
Bittersweet
Looped high
Rusts against
October blue;
Goldenrod
Growing too
Is dwarfed here
In the rocky field.
Whose daughter is that
With a stick peeled
And burrs caught
In her skirt's hem
Traipsing along
Unaware of them?
Burrs may prick her
If they please—
Timothy heads
May tap her knees—
She passes a turtle
And never sees;
A hostile twig
Swung to and fro
Jags her cheek
And she does not know.
She keeps step
To a strange hum:

Domino,
Dominum—
Amaverunt—
Futurus est—
Her cheeks flush
With a strange zest.

One need not mount
To find a view—
Mary Lyon
Descended to;
She came down
And I see her still
Coming down
From a rocky hill,
Coming down
With a book in her hand,
Thinking of women
In her land
That they could look
Through a telescope
As well as through
An embroidery hoop;
Could grasp as well
What a theorem means
As a recipe
For a pot of beans.
Gossip and parlor
Pieties,
Ladies' French
And melodian keys—
History—why not?—in exchange for these,
And to sit at the feet of Socrates.

And when she beckoned
I know they came
And took their places
In learning's name,
(Not necessarily
To make better mothers,
Any more
Than do their brothers

Stare an amoeba
In the face
To get a *paterfamilias*
Grace!)
But to find out
To the length of their care
What's protoplasm
And how does it fare;
And to find out
To the length of their will
What she brought down
From her rocky hill,
Serving her God
As she serves Him still
With a book in her hand
For a starved race,
And the look that a trained mind
Gives to the face.

Mary Lyon
By your Willow Ware,
By the Paris sashes
You bade them prepare
(Which *had* to be
The blue at noon,
Seen past green leaves,
Of a sky in June,
Now slowly faded
In trunks that moulder)
To tie delight
To a graduate's shoulder,
I know you longed
To have things right,
To have things right
And even rare,
But this was not
Your deepest care,
And if you folded
Your turban awry,
And failed to figure
Modishly,
You had distinction

In your eye
From notions strong
And sinewy;
Your mind could pull
A handsome stroke;
A word from you
And effort woke,—
Though you stepped down
From a country hill
It woke for you—
Pray it always will
Wherever you bow
Your cap's white crest
At a library table
Among the rest,
Your cheeks flushed
With a strange zest.

Hills that are green turn plum-color, then saffron,
Then slate again, re-powdered with the snow,
Till at their roots the wide Connecticut
Dampens the willows, and the oaks let go
The letter for the life that everywhere
Forsythia tries to featherstitch in air,
Or poplars spell with catkins on the walk.
Then ferns in woods with question marks displayed
Wait for the spring to end his lecture-talk,
Although he never *tells* them: they're so bright
They all can get the answers overnight
By just unfolding. That's the way to do it,
And maybe ferns were the first things that knew it,
Etching the delicate proof in chalk or coal
As Raphael recorded it in paint,
Euclid in law, Spinoza in the soul.
But first, of course, the right amount of rains
Must set the green blood spinning through the veins
Or else the truth's forever unrevealed
And looks more like closed gentians in a field
Than ferns, or sunflowers that show their seed.
One thinks of this and of the greater good
The day one sees an academic hood
Out airing on the line, with wind-whipped gown

And a gold tassel fallen on the grass.
For this was what our founder understood;
She said: "There is no gift without desire";
"One must not light an artificial fire."
It was of this she made her teachers sure—
And therefore, *gaudeamus igitur!*

For a hundred years your health, Mount Holyoke,
Has been your teachers. Teaching makes the school.
Two gallant Marys bred your quality.
One of your lines descends from Agassiz.
That prince of teachers, standing in the hay,
While barn-swallows flew round and round his head
Expounded wonders from a pail of fish,—
And Lydia Shattuck listened. None the less
Clapp, Jewett, Stevens, founts of your success
Prove it again: that teaching makes the school.
Your health, Mount Holyoke—those who know the rule,
Text, method, fundamentals, but profess
A college is a place where someone learns
Unfolding his own answers, like the ferns.
—ROBERTA TEALE SWARTZ

BENEDICTION

The benediction was pronounced by the Reverend Henry David Gray of South Hadley.

And now the God of all grace Who calls us to follow in the great procession of noble souls enlighten, guide and strengthen us in every high endeavor. To Him be honor, glory, dominion and power, world without end. Amen.

The ceremonies ended at twelve forty-five o'clock.

LUNCHEONS FOR GUESTS

The College entertained at luncheon on Saturday the official delegates of institutions and of alumnae clubs and classes and a large number of other guests. The head table and the speakers were on the platform of Wilbur Hall with a charming background of dogwood and palms. The table decorations of Japanese anemones helped to counteract with their bright colors the dull effect of a clouded sky.

Overflow luncheons in Mary Brigham, Safford, Porter, Mead and North and South Rockefeller Halls made possible the extension of college hospitality to include nearly one thousand guests.

The Alumnae Association provided a buffet luncheon in the great tent where fifteen hundred were served. Loud speakers in different buildings carried the speeches from Wilbur Hall to campus listeners and the radio broadcast to friends elsewhere.

PRESIDENT WOOLLEY: Friends: In behalf of all your hosts and hostesses, Trustees, Faculty, Alumnae, and the Undergraduates, we wish to tell you how much pleasure you have given us all by your presence, and to say a few words as our good-bye and Godspeed.

Although the student body is also hostess, I have asked one of the undergraduates to have a part in our program, Mary Tuttle, of the Senior Class, and Chairman of the Judicial Board of our Community Government. Mary Tuttle.

MARY ELVIN TUTTLE, CLASS OF 1937

Representing the Undergraduates

President Woolley and friends of Mount Holyoke: I think I know how the little acorn feels when it looks up at the mighty oak tree.

Many of you have heard perhaps of the new calendar in effect at Mount Holyoke this year. It is based on the day as a unit and time is reckoned from the two memorable days, May 7 and 8, and are labeled B.C. and A.C., before and after Centennial. We really hadn't put much faith in our new calendar, however, until we heard secretly that our professors were adhering to it and had abandoned the academic calendar in preference to the A.C., B.C. scheme. That to us proved its worth.

When President Woolley asked me a few weeks ago (B.C.) if I would represent the student body at this luncheon meeting and would say a few words in their behalf, my first impulse was to drop everything and run as far away from South Hadley as I could. Then my thoughts carried me to this luncheon, and I began to anticipate the opportunity which was offered me of meeting and hearing first hand the greetings of so many of our distinguished guests and the task seemed to become less and less impossible, at least from the point of view of my own desires. It really is, however, most difficult to express to you in a very few minutes the great significance of the Centennial to Mount Holyoke's present undergraduate body.

The actual experience is perhaps the most thrilling of all our undergraduate days. The preparation for our small part in the greater program has given us the deeper insight into the meaning of our hundred years of history and the afterglow of this outward expression will indeed be an inspiration to us all. It has been most interesting to watch the growth of enthusiasm on the part of the students from the time actual Centennial plans were begun. When the first Chapel Service was scheduled to announce tentative program plans it was the idea of some of the students that attendance at this meeting be required for all, but we soon found that it was not only unnecessary to require attendance at future Centennial meetings but rather our problem was to provide a seat for everyone who came, so great was the enthusiasm to hear every last bit of news to be released regarding plans for the event. Perhaps the height of student interest was expressed, however, when the Chairman of the early morning Frolic Committee rather timidly asked for a group of thirty-six to dance gaily around a maypole at seven o'clock in the morning and received over two hundred favorable replies to her request. And when people can be enthusiastic about Mount Holyoke's historical background at seven in the morning, there seems to be little need for further production of evidence concerning their interest in the celebration of their Alma Mater.

Some one once told me of a man who had lived in Washington all his life. The story goes that one day while on a tour of the city with some friends to whom he was showing the sights, he asked for directions to one of the important government buildings only to find that he was standing on its very steps. And so it is often with us at Mount Holyoke. We really feel we are a part of our College and yet little do we realize its greater significance to the world at large, what it has meant for the education and the furtherance of women's activity in the universal scheme, the part it has played in the fight for peace and in the establishment of international relationships throughout the world, and the rôle it has had in training women to make the world a better and happier place in which to live. A celebration such as this has given to us as students now a reason for the pride which we have in being a part of Mount Holyoke and its cause. It has made us realize as nothing else could the greater things which lie ahead and has brought to our consciousness the ideal laid down, shall we say, by our foremothers.

If I am in any way to express the thoughts that I know we as students should like expressed at this meeting, I should like to attempt the impossible again and in some small way express the pride we have every time our thoughts are turned to the name of President Woolley. I think we can often glean much from the most humble of examples and I should like to leave with you just two incidents which I think express in a small degree our affection for Miss Woolley. It is Miss Woolley's practice to lead the Chapel Service on Tuesday and Friday mornings of each week but with the overcrowded schedules of this second semester it has been impossible for her to be with us as often as her usual schedule permits. And so we eagerly watch the weekly calendar hopeful that Miss Woolley is to lead one of the Chapel Services of the week. And no matter what the substitution for Miss Woolley's absence, though there is complete understanding, there seems to be an air of disappointment which nothing can wave, save Miss Woolley herself.

On a rather busy evening during the winter term it was suggested that we might wander down to the President's House during the early evening to serenade Miss Woolley. Our song leader felt some anxiety as to the size of the group which would be there because of numerous other events and meetings scheduled for the same night. I really am hesitant to guess at the number of meetings that waited that evening and went off schedule, for I would wager that well over 99 and 44/100 of the student body were standing along Miss Woolley's drive, singing their praises to her.

These are but two very humble incidents to express the magnetic personality which has drawn the love and loyalty of ten thousand Mount Holyoke women and countless others under the influence of the outstanding figure of Mount Holyoke's Centennial celebration. In these days and years which follow (A.C., according to our new calendar) it will be the figure of Mary E. Woolley which will hold for us the summation of the significance of our presence here, just as it has been the personality of Mary Lyon in these preceding one hundred years.

PRESIDENT WOOLLEY: When I was an undergraduate in the Women's College at Brown University, I remember that the College Annual asked concerning Malcolm Chase, then a tennis champion, "What is the matter with Malcolm? Nothing except that he has to put his hat on with a shoe horn."

That is Mount Holyoke's condition in thinking of her Daughter Colleges. We are very proud of our five Daughter Colleges. Two of them are in foreign countries—the Huguenot, in South Africa, and the International Institute at Madrid, today going through such a tragic experience. Three are in this country, Lake Erie at Painesville, Ohio; Western, at Oxford, Ohio; Mills College on the Pacific Coast.

President Reinhardt, who has crossed the continent to be with us on our birthday will speak in behalf of the Daughter Colleges. President Reinhardt.

AURELIA HENRY REINHARDT

Representing the Daughter Colleges

President Woolley and friends of Mount Holyoke: It is the fashion today in the average human family to disregard the generations, their development of the one from the other, the dependence of the one upon the other, the responsibility of the one for the other. As mothers persist in being sisters to their daughters, and playmates of their grandchildren, we find the terms of blood kinship carried out of the family into many group relationships.

So, today, institutions of education become members of a human family, in our terms of reference and in realization of relationships. We find among them a parenthood of ideals, inspirations, affections. We find among them brotherhood and sisterhood in a contemporaneousness of enterprise, discipline, goal and achievement. We find an academic family tree, growing steadily through the years. As in human genealogy we find some institutions indifferent to origins, some concerned only with early roots, and some interested in the value of the annual harvest, as also in the latest horticultural methods to improve the quality of fruit.

Personally, I like analogies, and on this occasion, I shall use one that arises from tree life, and expresses even better than the family tree, the dynamics of the educational process.

On the western shores of North America grows the Sequoia. Not only in architectural nobility, in unquenchable verdure, and in its incalculable age does it stand without comparison among trees. More than any other growing thing it has the secret of life. It is primordial in its ability to preserve and to reproduce itself. Life continues in uninterrupted vigor through planted seed or twig or branch; through sprouted roots moving sunward or through the boles under the russet-colored bark.

Institutions of education are like the redwood in their exhaustless power to conserve and recreate mental life.

Witness Mount Holyoke, mother of women's colleges, as on her honored hundredth anniversary, her daughters salute her across the world and across the century of her years.

Since she came into being in 1837, she has lived through her children, through their achievements as individuals, and through the institutions which they in turn planted, or to which they gave their talents. Seed grew to sapling. Many saplings make a forest.

Mount Holyoke has seen some thousands of English-speaking folk on the Atlantic Coast, farmers, fishers, shipbuilders, merchants, send westward their children and their children's children, to fell forests, to lay railroads, to build factories, to develop cities—wives, mothers, and teachers of these pioneers called Mount Holyoke Alma Mater.

There came the long heart-breaking struggle of the Civil War, to bring an end to chattel slavery; to bring South and North into economic and political accord. No group of women were so numerous, so devoted, so ready to attack the problems of insurmountable difficulty among helpless Negro populations as the disciples of Mary Lyon.

As the years passed and millions of non-English-speaking folk brought their talents and their industry to the maturing of an emerging technical civilization with its human triumphs and human tragedies, from Mount Holyoke came intelligent women who through school and church, club and community enterprise, playground and library strove to meet diverse and conflicting human needs.

As early as 1850, Susan Mills had begun that educational work in Batticotta and in Hawaii, which was to carry her to California, where for forty-seven years she worked with contagious enthusiasm to establish a college for women above San Francisco Bay. Today it carries her revered name.

By 1853, Susan Mills' friend, Helen Peabody, began at Western College in Ohio a parallel task to which she devoted her life for over three decades.

By 1859 Lydia Sessions at Painesville in the Western Reserve was the first of four Mount Holyoke graduates to found a unique academic dynasty which has guided Lake Erie College through an educational youth to an enviable strength and authority among contemporary colleges.

By 1871 Alice Gordon Gulick had carried into Spain that devotion to learning and that democratic faith in learning that was to waken Spanish women to new uses of the mind and of time. The work which she inaugurated was to become after arduous years the International Institute for Girls in Spain.

By 1873 Abbie P. Ferguson and Anna E. Bliss were co-founders in Wellington, Cape Province, South Africa, of a school which became a system of schools, which developed branch academies and a training school for teachers, and which capped its atonishing creativity by bringing into existence the only woman's college in the Union of South Africa.

Long before statesmen were thinking in terms of a World Court, a League of Nations, or a Pact of Paris, Mount Holyoke was dedicated to bringing harmony out of world discord, and to finding kinship in races that called themselves enemies.

It is in the tradition of the great college whose hundredth birthday is today our theme, that the Daughter Colleges and the academic households throughout the world salute Mount Holyoke and her President. It is in the horizon of so inclusive a task that President Woolley led the College of which she has been President since the turn of the century. We rejoice that in our modern complexity President Woolley keeps her serene faith in unity; that amid contemporary animosity she teaches and exemplifies friendship; that amid ignorances and prejudices she seeks understanding; that in the din of munition-making, she seeks disarmament. We rejoice in her idealistic leadership.

What woman of today has given of herself so wholly, wrought

so indefatigably, traveled and taught so unselfishly, as President Mary E. Woolley? I pronounce her name with affection and reverence that her daughters everywhere may hear it linked with their Alma Mater, Mount Holyoke, and their prophetic founder, Mary Lyon, in her service through women for international comity.

PRESIDENT WOOLLEY: Among the good fortunes which have come to me in my life, was my clergyman father with his fund of good stories. I remember the story of a brother clergyman who was bitterly opposed to having a Women's Missionary Society in his church and, when it was finally carried against opposition, said with emphasis: "Well, anyway, I am always going to be present, for there is no telling what those women if left to themselves will ask the Lord for!"

Early in the history of Mount Holyoke, there was a picnic on one of the mountains by which we are girded, attended by the students of Amherst College as well as by the students of Mount Holyoke.

When the toasts came at the conclusion of this picnic, an Amherst student responded for the Seminary girls. Since his father was a trustee of Mount Holyoke, the appropriateness was apparent, and a perfectly decorous and modest way of responding for the young ladies was carried through.

We have many brother colleges, we are often impressed by that fact on the campus of Mount Holyoke. There is no brother quite so near, as far as mileage is concerned, as Amherst. It has been near many times in other ways as well, and we are glad today to have the opportunity of introducing President King of Amherst College, who will speak to us for the brother colleges. President King.

STANLEY KING

Representing the Brother Colleges

President Woolley and friends of Mount Holyoke: I am very happy to be here today. As you know, I am here in my representative capacity. I represent the brothers of Mount Holyoke. There are older brothers and younger brothers. As Mount Holyoke does not mind confessing its age of one hundred, I am prepared to confess that for the day I am one hundred and sixteen years old, and I am speaking today as an elder brother, Miss Woolley, as your elder brother. In that capacity I bring to Mount Holyoke the congratulations of her brother colleges, congratulations on the one hundred years that have passed, and best wishes for the years that lie ahead.

But I would be untrue to the trust that is placed in me today if I did not speak also for hundreds, even thousands of alumni of these brother colleges who during the past hundred years have married graduates of Mount Holyoke. I wonder if Mount Holyoke realizes what she is doing in extra-curricular education, for each of those men has continued his education throughout his life under the tutelage of a Mount Holyoke graduate.

And then I want to speak for our undergraduates. I address these remarks to you, Miss Tuttle. Our undergraduates, not only the undergraduates of Amherst but the undergraduates of other men's colleges for a hundred or two hundred miles' radius around here, send their affectionate greetings to the undergraduates of Mount Holyoke.

It is true, I think, that if you asked the deans of Amherst College they would say that Mount Holyoke had added to their burdens. None the less, I think in all sincerity that Mount Holyoke and her sister colleges are educating our young men socially in a way that we could never educate them on the campuses of our own colleges.

That fact has not been given enough consideration, it seems to me, in the deliberations which have accompanied this centenary, for the social education of the boys in our colleges is due very largely to their contacts with the undergraduates in the women's colleges.

Mount Holyoke and Amherst are sprung from the same soil; the same sturdy, God-fearing, thrifty and austere New England stock produced us both. And as I read the story of the founding of Mount Holyoke, I am reminded very much of the incidents in our founding.

Deacon Porter and Deacon Safford who helped Mary Lyon in the early days of Mount Holyoke have their counterparts in the men who assisted Amherst College during its early days. Mount Holyoke was founded one hundred years ago. I wonder if we realize the difficulties that existed in 1837 and that faced Mary Lyon.

We are preoccupied with the difficulties that we have been facing during the late depression, but 1837 was one of the most critical years that our country faced. It was in that year that Mary Lyon chose to found this College. There had been unprecedented prosperity, and then a financial collapse in London followed by a complete collapse in this country. Cotton dropped from twenty cents to ten cents, and flour went up to twelve dollars and fifty cents a barrel. There were riots in New York, and we had external difficulties. We had a Seminole war going on in Florida, trouble on the Mexican frontier, and we had very serious trouble on the Canadian frontier which came near embroiling us with Great Britain. It was that year that Mary Lyon founded this College.

In reading some of the reminiscences written eighty years ago by a President of Amherst, I came across this phrase of Mary Lyon's. She said: "It is one of the nicest intellectual operations to distinguish between the impossible and the very difficult." Every college president realizes the truth of that statement, but I think some of us will also realize that she made what was apparently an impossible task a merely very difficult task when she founded this College.

And to you, Miss Woolley, I bring the greetings of your colleagues in other colleges. You have been President of Mount Holyoke longer than any of us have been at the head of our institutions. You came to Mount Holyoke in 1900 and, speaking again as your elder brother, I will say I remember very distinctly that year 1900 when you became President of Mount Holyoke, because it was in that year that Brown University and Amherst College each conferred upon you an honorary doctorate. So far as Amherst College was concerned, that was the first honorary degree ever conferred upon a woman by Amherst College. I remember that Commencement. Our trustees in their wisdom did not select me to hang the hood upon your shoulders. I was still a sub-freshman, not having yet entered Amherst College. But as I look over our colleagues in other colleges, both those that are here and those that are not here, it seems to me that the man whom we look to as having been president of his institution longer than any of us can remember officially is President Butler, and you, Miss Woolley, became President of Mount Holyoke two years before President Butler became President of Columbia University.

Mary Lyon has become a symbol for the education, the higher education of women, and Miss Woolley in her lifetime has lived to see herself become such a symbol, for Mary Lyon and Mary Woolley are associated in the minds of all of us with the education of women on the college level.

In closing, I say to Mount Holyoke and to you, Miss Woolley, paraphrasing the words of the Bible, may you both live forever!

PRESIDENT WOOLLEY: President King modestly refrained from reference to the manifold debts that Mount Holyoke owes Amherst. Mary Lyon might never have founded Mount Holyoke had she not received a large part of her education and inspiration from Amherst professors who were keenly interested in this young and able girl.

From the beginning they helped as trustees, as lecturers, in numerous ways. For years Dr. Hitchcock was one of the members of the Board upon whom I depended.

I am sure you have begun to realize that this is really a family party of daughters, sisters and brothers. The next speaker is related in so many ways that I hardly know which one to choose. Dean Morriss was one of our faculty; is the dean of the college from which I hold my own degrees in course; and now claims all college women as daughters since she is President of the American Association of University Women. Dean Morriss.

MARGARET SHOVE MORRISS
Representing Brown University

President Woolley, honored guests, and friends of Mount Holyoke College: When President Woolley asked me to speak on this great occasion representing Brown University and Pembroke College, she pointed out to me that it was going to be a family occasion, that there would be a great deal of emphasis on family relationships, so I thought that somehow or other I must fit our College into the family situation.

She told me that there would be greetings from a brother college, from a sister college, from a daughter college. "But what," she said, "is the relationship of Brown University to Mount Holyoke? A sister, or a cousin or an aunt?"

She was not quite sure, and neither was I, but I have since then tried to work out the relationship which Brown holds to Mount Holyoke. Old Brown University, mother of so many, is the Alma Mater of your President. Surely that is almost the same as being the mother of this College, because it has certainly been the mother of the builder of the modern Mount Holyoke through more than one-third of its whole history.

Brown is Alma Mater to Miss Woolley and, shall we say, perhaps, mother-in-law to Mount Holyoke College. As such a close relative it brings to you warm greetings and congratulations today.

President Woolley is one of the greatest of Brown's long list of illustrious alumni. Legends grow up about great people even in their lifetime, and already such legends have been clustering around Miss Woolley's name in our community.

There is a story that I heard from a fellow classmate of hers which is still being told somewhat ruefully, I must admit. Miss Woolley was the only woman in a class of men—I think it may have been one of Professor Jameson's classes. Of course, she sat modestly in a corner, as Pembroke College has always known the proper place of women. Questions went round the class and were answered not at all to the professor's satisfaction. Finally he turned impatiently from the others and somewhat complacently to the modest student in the rear of the room, "Now, Miss Woolley," he said, "perhaps *you* will tell us what really happened on this occasion!"

There is also a legend that Miss Woolley was actually responsible for the founding of Pembroke College, that it was her desire for a college education and her fine mentality which so impressed President Andrews, our founder, that he convinced the Corporation of Brown University that the women of Rhode Island should have opportunities for a college education at Brown. So examinations were opened, classes started for Miss Woolley and other women, and Pembroke College began.

The story goes that these classes had to be held sometimes in the office of the President of the University, because the only other room available for the women students did not have any gas light.

Miss Woolley completed her work for the Bachelor's degree in three years, one of the first two women to receive a degree in course at Brown University. By the time she had graduated, education for women had become an accepted fact at Brown, due not only to her pioneering courage but also to her outstanding ability. She had proved in her own person that women could succeed in higher education.

It is an old story today, but it was very important then, and Pembroke College owes more to Miss Woolley and the other women of her time than it can possibly put into words. She set a standard for women that I am afraid we have never yet equalled. But after all, she made us "hitch our wagon to a star"—and that is how it should be.

Brown realizes with pride that President Woolley has justified the high promise she showed in those early days. Everywhere she has touched the education of women she has helped to gain new opportunities for her sex. As inspiring teacher first at Wheaton and then at Wellesley, she led young people to a new interest in things of the mind. As President of the American Association of University Women she helped to give to the college women of America new standards for continuing education in their own lives after they had finished their formal instruction, and also for service to education in their communities.

The first woman in the United States to be appointed to an international commission as one of the United States delegates to the Disarmament Conference at Geneva, Miss Woolley opened new paths for women in the service of their country. Incidentally, I would like to repeat something that I heard about Miss Woolley in Geneva. An American woman who is a high official in the English League of Nations Union, told me that Lord Robert Cecil once said that he thought Miss Woolley would be a sort of ornamental personage in the American delegation, because it was a very desirable thing to appoint a woman. But instead of that he found to his surprise she was the best informed member of the delegation, that he could count on her always for most intelligent co-operation on every issue. Of course, we could have told Lord Robert that would be the case, but it did seem a surprise to him.

But the supreme example of Miss Woolley's accomplishment lies around us today in the modern Mount Holyoke in whose success we are rejoicing. I have been fortunate enough to have spent a number of years of my life on the faculty of Mount Holyoke, and since those years I have always felt as if I belong to the College. And may I digress to say how very happy and proud I am today to feel that for the future I am really one of the alumnae of Mount Holyoke College.

Because of those early associations with Mount Holyoke, which are so dear to me, I have known it for a long time. I remember gas-lighted classrooms in Mount Holyoke, too, in old Williston Hall. When the thunderstorms came up and the rooms grew dark before their time, we had to stand on the seat of one of the chairs and light the gas so that we could see to go on with our lectures. That was old Williston Hall a long time ago. I rejoice now in the sight of Clapp Laboratory, the new library, the really marvelous increase in material equipment since I was here.

Mount Holyoke College has always had the highest academic standards for its students, and the ablest of faculties, but in all the years it has gone from strength to strength under the wise guidance of our illustrious daughter whose life has been primarily dedicated to the service of this College.

On behalf of Brown University and Pembroke College, I congratulate Mount Holyoke on its good fortune, on its great leadership in recent times, and on its splendid accomplishments for women during all the past one hundred years.

May I close with the words of President Faunce of Brown University written to Miss Woolley twenty-five years ago on the occasion of the Seventy-fifth Anniversary of this College. Those words were remarkably true at the time, and I am sure they will be equally true in the next one hundred years.

"This date," said President Faunce, "is not only a terminus but a threshold, and good wine will come at the end of the feast."

PRESIDENT WOOLLEY: Mount Holyoke has today many sisters. It had a sister in 1837, Wheaton Seminary, then two years old, later Wheaton College, to whom it has always been bound by the closest of ties. It has a sister just across the river, a sister with whom it rejoices to stand shoulder to shoulder, and not "cold shoulder to cold shoulder," as Katharine Bates once wittily said of two other colleges.

I am glad that President Neilson is here this afternoon to speak in behalf of Mount Holyoke's sister colleges. President Neilson.

WILLIAM ALLAN NEILSON
Representing the Sister Colleges

Miss Woolley, guests of Mount Holyoke: I cannot pretend to be here as a representative of the sister colleges through their choice; I was selected, I think, by Miss Woolley. And since my sister colleges had no responsibility for my being here, I feel no responsibility to them in what I may say about them.

I know, however, that they join with me very heartily in bringing to you on this occasion, congratulations and best wishes for the future. On such occasions one is constantly led, as speech follows speech, to compare the institutions and try to define the individual personality of the one we are celebrating.

As I listened to the speeches this morning, and as I listened to them this afternoon, my mind has constantly been trying to outline the individuality of Mount Holyoke as it is distinguished from the rest of us.

I think of it chiefly in comparison with the inner group of sister colleges, the five colleges that work especially close together—Vassar, Bryn Mawr, Wellesley and Smith. One fact that does not seem to have been touched upon today has occurred to me, namely, that there was a difference in the founding of Mount Holyoke, separating it from these other four colleges.

In the case of the other four, the founder of the college was a man or woman of means who had an idea about the importance of the education of women, and who left funds for the furtherance of it. These are the financial, material founders of these institutions, Dr. Taylor, Dr. Durant, Sofia Smith, and Matthew Vassar.

Then there came other founders, the intellectual and spiritual founders of these colleges—sometimes more than one. The real founders of Bryn Mawr are Miss Thomas and Miss Park; the real founders of Vassar are Dr. Taylor and Dr. McCracken; the real founders of Wellesley—although in this case the material founder had more to say—were a whole series of presidents down through Miss Pendleton and Miss McAfee; the real founder of Smith was Mr. Seelye.

But in the case of Mount Holyoke, the two were one. There was no rich man or rich woman who found Mary Lyon to do the first job as President. She conceived the whole project. She found the means, she became the President. She laid the foundation, and she laid it all. And perhaps it is because of this double function of hers that her personality has affected Mount Holyoke more profoundly than was the case in regard to any of the other colleges.

No one person during the first two generations of the existence of Mount Holyoke Seminary, no one person in any of the other colleges has such an exclusive claim to have drawn the lines on which it was to move and given it the spirit that animated it.

Yet Mount Holyoke, too, has two founders. Mary Lyon, after all, was the founder of Mount Holyoke Seminary, the founder in the sense in which I have been speaking of the other colleges. Modern Mount Holyoke College is Miss Woolley, and that is what today most of us regard as Mount Holyoke.

Mary Lyon is a half-legendary, heroic, saintly figure, beginning her great activity for this institution a hundred years ago. We have read about her, and Mount Holyoke has kept her name hallowed.

But Miss Woolley is a real person. With her we have worked;

we have heard her speak; we have seen her accomplish her great achievement. She is fortunate in being able to come to this point where she sees her College fully abreast of all the institutions of its kind throughout the world, and to have known that it was she who thought of it in these terms, whose keen appreciation of forward movements has set new standards, whose acuteness in the selection of staff has built up its distinguished faculty, and whose spirit, extraordinarily profound and broad, have given Mount Holyoke the quality that it has today.

For that reason, she deserves a unique kind of congratulation, and it is out of the intimate knowledge that sisters have that I bring congratulations to her institution today.

Mothers and daughters love each other; brothers and sisters tolerate each other; but sisters know each other.

We know Mount Holyoke, we of the sister colleges. We watch every movement. We know all of what she professes and how she lives up to what she professes, and it is out of this fullness of knowledge that we bring our heartfelt congratulations on the past and our cordial wishes for the next one hundred years.

PRESIDENT WOOLLEY: May I say as we close our program today that we of Mount Holyoke are very grateful to you all for the way in which you have made our Centenary birthday party an inspiration. We appreciate your coming. We are made both humble and proud by what you have said. We value your confidence; it means a great deal to us, more than you will ever know. I can only say, thank you all!

We hope that you are not flying—literally or figuratively— away from the campus. We hope that the Glee Club will attract you to the chapel, and the Goldman Band to the auditorium.

We say, Thank you! from the depths of our hearts.

The meeting adjourned at three twenty-five o'clock.

CONCERT BY THE GOLDMAN BAND

The gray chilly air of Saturday afternoon did not deter Centennial guests from attending the outdoor concert by the Goldman Band. It was open to the general public and many people from South Hadley and the surrounding towns came to hear in person the well-known conductor whose radio concerts they had often enjoyed. At four-thirty, Mr. Goldman stepped to the front of the laurel-hung platform, and was enthusiastically greeted by an audience which filled the center section and a part of the side sections of the large South Campus auditorium. The program was as follows:

March, "Builders of America". . . . . . . *Goldman*
Overture, "Mignon" . . . . *Thomas*
"Unfinished Symphony," first movement . . . *Schubert*
Excerpts from "Carmen" . . . . *Bizet*

Excerpts from "Faust" . . . . *Gounod*
Cornet solo, "Irish Fantasy" . . . . *Rogers*
Leonard B. Smith, Cornetist
Marches
  "Children's March" . . . . *Goldman*
  "Bugles and Drums" . . . . *Goldman*
  "On the Mall". . . . . *Goldman*
Grand March, "University" . . . . *Goldman*

Mount Holyoke College is indebted to the generosity of Mrs. William G. Dwight of Holyoke and the *Holyoke Transcript-Telegram* for the music furnished by the Goldman Band during the Centenary Days. This gift is made as a tribute to President Woolley, Professor Hammond, and Helen Clarke Dwight, a student at the Seminary in its first year and the mother of the late William G. Dwight, Editor and owner of the *Transcript* for nearly fifty years.

SUPPLEMENT

THE ADMINISTRATION OF A CENTENARY

IT is truly not an exaggeration to say that Mount Holyoke's Centennial was in preparation for twenty-five years—from the close of its dress rehearsal, the Seventy-fifth Anniversary. An aura of plans and aims—conceived idly or jokingly, no doubt, at first—began to invest *annum domini* 1937 with a somewhat glorified character. There were vague plans for the celebration itself, for permanent improvements in the College. Gradually the projects grew serious, and then purposeful. Three years of organized work were required for their fruition.

The Central Centennial Committee of ten members, later increased to twenty-two, representing trustees, administrative officers, faculty and alumnae, held its first meeting on May 23, 1934. On July 1, 1937, the Central Centennial Office was closed. Between those dates there grew up in South Hadley a complete and energetic administrative network.

The discussions of the May 1934 meeting included in some form every feature of the final celebration. The Committee gave especial attention to the need of a history of the College. At its second meeting in October 1934 the subcommittee on Publications made several definite proposals; in May 1935 a distinguished scholar signed the contract for writing the *History of Mount Holyoke College*. This and the other Centennial publications are listed and described on pp. 144–46.

In June 1936 the important change of date of the Centenary from October to May, 1937, was voted, a change desired in order that the celebration might fall within the administration of President Woolley. In October 1936 as the volume of preparation became formidable, Miss Marion H. Barbour of New York, Mount Holyoke 1920, was appointed as full-time Executive Secretary of the Centennial Committee.

THE CENTRAL CENTENNIAL OFFICE

In November the familiar Community Government room in Student-Alumnae Hall became, under Miss Barbour's direction, the Central Centennial Office of manifold functions. All preparations under the Central Committee's jurisdiction were executed by subcommittees. It was the duty of the Central Office to call and record the meetings of these committees; to recommend to President Woolley the appointment of new committees; to furnish stenographic and clerical assistance; to approve all Maintenance Department orders involved; and to provide any other services necessary. The "other services" assumed large and interesting proportions, particularly those connected with invitations and hospitality.

INVITATIONS. Earlier in the year, under the painstaking direction of Miss Caroline B. Greene, an invitation list of nearly fourteen thousand names of individuals and institutions had been assembled. Of the individuals, ten thousand were, of course, Mount Holyoke alumnae. In the case of colleges and universities to be invited to send delegates, the limited capacity of our auditoriums made selection necessary. Learned societies and research foundations, libraries, junior colleges, and public and private schools were also represented on the list. The small sanctum in Student-Alumnae Hall which housed the file of these names became a vital branch of the Centennial Office.

In January the decorative preliminary announcement* was mailed to colleges and universities. Meanwhile the actual invitation, together with its various enclosures—a program of events, a list of hotel accommodations in the vicinity, and a reply card to be returned to the College—was drawn up and engraved. During February the invitations were addressed, those of alumnae by addressograph in the Alumnae Office, all others handwritten. Stamping and sorting for enclosure was a feverish session, but on the first of March the post-office carriers bore off

* See frontispiece.

in basketfuls some fourteen thousand thick white envelopes.

As replies came in new duties developed. Complete files of acceptances and regrets had to be maintained. The names of delegates, with their titles, positions, and the foundation dates of their institutions had to be assembled for the Chief Marshal and for the compiler of the program. A follow-up card checking the accuracy of this information as received had to go to each delegate. Last but not least the entertainment of official guests had to be provided for, a problem which led to the opening of yet another branch Centennial Office, that of the Secretary for Hospitality, Mrs. Lawrence C. Wellington of Amherst.

HOSPITALITY. The term "official guests" was used to indicate those to whom the College wished to extend hospitality, delegates, speakers, recipients of honorary degrees, trustees, alumnae class and club representatives, and various friends of the College, including, of course, the wives or husbands of these individuals. As many as possible of these official guests, in particular the alumnae representatives, were to be entertained on the campus, the students in the larger houses vacating the first and second floors and taking their meals at earlier hours to make this arrangement possible. For the rest the Committee had secured the hospitality of homes in the vicinity, local committees under the general chairmanship of Dean Cheek having canvassed the surrounding towns. So gracious was the response of our neighbors that in all 125 homes from Springfield to Northampton and Amherst were opened to Centennial guests.

Under Mrs. Wellington's direction the Hospitality Office assumed the nice task of assigning guests to these hospitable homes. As acceptances were received the office entered into individual correspondence with each guest and each hostess. It was a task involving not only judicious selection, but an infinitude of detail regarding transportation, times of arrival, special needs, and a constantly shifting margin of additional guests who planned to accompany the delegates and others. A file of all this information had to be maintained and kept abreast of changes in guests' plans; this was the master file later used in the preparation of tickets and the registration of guests. In addition the names of guests who accepted invitations to the luncheon of Saturday, May eighth, were filed by this office for the Luncheon Committee's use. During the Centenary Days, the Hospitality Office also managed the fleet of official cars, driven principally by students, that met official guests at the stations and conveyed them to the College.

Preparations for the reception of the alumnae were being carried on by the Alumnae Office. Alumnae everywhere had talked celebration, lived it in anticipation, and planned their attendance for a period of years, but not until their acceptances began to pour into the office was the full extent of their interest realized.

The canvass of the hospitality committees had located, as well as rooms for the official guests, hundreds of rooms in hotels, tourist houses, and private homes for alumnae accommodations. These reservations were carefully assigned by the Alumnae Office as applications were received. Many other alumnae visited friends, or made their own reservations without reference to the Alumnae Office. Members of the oldest classes, as well as the official class and club representatives, were entertained on the campus.

COMMITTEES. Meanwhile, the general functions of the Central Office were continued. Many new committees were created. In all, 41 committees worked on the Centennial, totaling 306 members, drawn from faculty, faculty wives, staff, trustees, students, alumnae, and friends outside the College, together with a very few professional advisers; the full list is contained in the Appendix. Some of these committee names are self-explanatory; others merit a brief description.

CAMPUS PREPARATIONS. The indefatigable Committee on Campus Preparations supervised details from the beautiful illumination of the campus to the costuming of the student guides in their tailored white dresses with blue accessories.

COSTUMES. The Costume Committee on the Garden Party, with the help of the Central Office, requested, collected, catalogued, altered to fit student wearers, and returned some five hundred authentic costumes loaned by alumnae and friends.

TICKETS. The Tickets Committee, together with the Centennial Office staff, prepared and addressed an envelope containing tickets and informational material for every expected guest. Since tickets were divided into major groups, differentiated by color, indicating to which hall they would admit in case of rain, this problem was one of almost incredible intricacy.

STUDENT ACTIVITY. Student activity was under the direction of a Student Central Centennial Committee, which held its first meeting on December fifth before the fire in the Mary Lyon House at Buckland, a group whose intelligent enthusiasm penetrated the campus to a truly remarkable degree. The Committee supervised student publications, arranged a series of four chapel talks by campus and outside speakers to stimulate interest in college history, and extended invitations to the Daughter Colleges to send student delegates. As committee members, as guides, ushers, and hostesses, as assistants in Departmental Exhibits, as choir members, or as actors in the Pantomime or Dance Recital, very nearly the whole student body actively participated in the celebration. After the Centennial, a committee of students under the leadership of the Chairman of Community, Rosamond Frame, sealed a box inscribed "Centenary of Mount Holyoke College, 1837–1937, to be opened at the Bicentenary," and placed it in the vault in Williston Memorial Library. The box contained a prophecy concerning the United States a hundred years hence, the outgrowth of work done by a discussion group in American history.

ALTERNATIVE PLANS. Through the plans ran a constant refrain "In case of rain." The South Campus auditorium, seating five thousand people, with the silver-painted platforms constructed on the east side of Skinner Hall, was planned as the scene of major events; but the misfortunes befalling a brilliant celebration not long before warned us to be prepared to move them indoors. Since Chapin, our largest indoor auditorium, seats only thirteen hundred people, relay systems were provided by the Eastern Radio Company to carry the events from Chapin to amplifiers in Mary Lyon Chapel, Pratt Music Hall, and Williston Memorial Library.

SERVICE AGENCIES. As the celebration neared, a multitude of miscellaneous duties arose. Travel arrangements from Hongkong, London, and American cities had to be made for speakers and other guests. Conferences filled the calendar—with the caterers, the H. J. Seiler Company of Boston; with the Byron Jackson Company of Boston; and the Bray Awning Company of Holyoke; with the manager of the Goldman Band; with the heads of the Springfield and Holyoke Street Railway Companies, whose courteous co-operation made possible transportation schedules to accommodate our guests; with representatives of the State Police, whose efficient handling of the traffic problem minimized the confusion of the Centennial Days; with the engineers of the General Electric Company and the Eastern Radio Company. Groups of student volunteers joined us for large clerical tasks.

ARRIVAL AND REGISTRATION. Before we could believe it the celebration was upon us. At two-thirty on Thursday afternoon, May sixth, the first Centennial guest approached the Information Desk in Skinner Hall. To us in the Centennial Offices the celebration materialized not so much in the actual events already described in this book, as in the blur of activity that centered for three days on that amazingly transformed academic stronghold.

In one room a corps of village boys waited to carry or check luggage. Another room was a Gift Shop, selling Centennial Publications and souvenir articles provided by various alumnae clubs; here Dr. Dole demonstrated her famous hand-weaving. Still another room served as a post office for incoming and outgoing mail. Arriving guests streamed by toward the Registration Rooms where their tickets and programs awaited them. A corridor table did a flourishing business in the Centennial Supplements of the *Holyoke Transcript-Telegram;* another with busily ringing telephones supplied schedules of excursions into the Mary Lyon country.

INFORMATION DESK. Center of all the activity was the Information Desk, in charge of four Centennial Office secretaries and relays of the two hundred student guides. Here we were prepared, or hoped we were, to answer any and all questions about campus, program, transportation, and the like; to mention a village nursery school where children might be cared for; to direct hungry guests to thirty-nine restaurants in South Hadley and surrounding towns, or to the campus sandwich booths operated by the Outing Club, or to the chicken supper served by the ladies of the village church. Here too was a master file of all registered guests—the registration card for each guest being sent from the Registration Rooms to the Information Desk as soon as the guest had signed it on arrival.

NUMBER OF GUESTS. Because of the fact that many guests in attendance failed to register though they had sent acceptances, and that many more who had neglected to answer their invitations arrived at the last moment, it is impossible to state accurately the number who attended the Centennial. A review of the reports submitted by the Alumnae Secretary and the Secretary for Hospitality indicates that about 4,348 people were on the campus at one time or another during the Centennial, divided as follows: faculty and staff, past and present, 226; student body, 980; alumnae, 2,200 (2,080 actually registered); non-alumnae, official and unofficial, 942 (882 actually registered). The official guests numbered 275, divided as follows: delegates of American colleges, universities, and theological seminaries, 177; delegates of foreign colleges and universities, 25; delegates of educational societies and foundations, 33; trustees, 20; recipients of honorary degrees, 20. The Secretary for Hospitality reports that 132 of these official guests were entertained in private homes, approximately 100 on campus, and 5, at their own request, in hotels. About 30 guests declined our hospitality because of other plans, and between 40 and 50 were residents of neighboring towns.

ALUMNAE ATTENDANCE. Perhaps it is not inappropriate here to mention the striking extent of the alumnae attendance. Ceremonial days have a way of playing upon uncommonly deep notes, of lending a new and appealing vitality to old memories and affections that have seemed long since forgotten. "If I have not given unmistakably the atmosphere of delight and excitement and unbounded pleasure in the Centenary," the Alumnae Secretary says in her report, "then I have fallen short of the actual fact."

Not since the Seventy-fifth had there been such an unbroken line of classes to visit the College at one time. Every class from 1872 through 1936 was represented, as well as 1861, 1868, and 1869 of the earlier group. Many classes held informal reunions with class meetings and picnics. Wherever the groups gathered, large or small, jubilee was the keynote. Many had not returned to the College for years, some not since graduation. As the hours of the two days passed, the gray air seemed peopled with a strangely dramatic chorus of voices—voices that hailed friends, that cried with surprise at the new sights, or with joy at the old. The sound of them translated the routines of an arduous year into human and oddly memorable terms which lingered rather hauntingly in the minds of all of us who had worked at preparing the Centennial.

Again before we could realize it, the tumult and the shouting had died. Facing an office filled with the inevitable debris of aftermath, we began to ask ourselves, a bit numbly, the questions one always asks oneself when a major effort is over. It was an immeasurable gratification to find answers to some of these questions in the countless gracious letters that poured in from participants in the celebration. We quote from a very few of these:

[From unofficial guests]

The whole occasion was one of perfect arrangement and achievement —a triumph of taste and beauty. It was, moreover, a magnificent tribute to you [President Woolley] personally and officially, as it should have been.

The days of your great Centennial will always remain among the exceptional experiences of my life. I felt the significance of the event very deeply . . . The beautiful scene of the garden party seemed to me the sort of thing we try to revive from quieter more gracious times—and here it was, part of our life today, with reminiscences of the past to give it value and importance. All of the days, every event, seemed handled so intelligently and ably. I just had a *beautiful* time!

[From delegates]

Like all your guests I want to thank you for a beautiful and memorable experience. It was all delightfully planned and carried out, and from the moment we reached the Springfield Station we were cared for in the most friendly and hospitable way. It was as if the keys of South Hadley and Mount Holyoke were presented on a velvet cushion to each one of us. Yet our faculty and alumnae and student hostesses did not seem overburdened. They were celebrating themselves, and apparently enjoying it.

The orderly way in which everything moved along—in spite of the fickle weather—the delightful hospitality which I enjoyed, and every other item so carefully handled deserve the warmest congratulations from all of your guests.

Please accept my warm thanks for the great courtesy shown me during my recent attendance at the memorable celebration, and an expression, unfortunately quite inadequate, of my admiration for the extremely efficient way in which the complicated details of the arrangements were carried out. It was a notable achievement in a notable program.

The whole affair was beautifully managed. I enjoyed every minute of it, and feel that I could easily put in another day looking at the interesting exhibits. I very much appreciated being entertained in a dormitory . . . The girls who acted as hostesses carried their part with admirable finish. I have no doubt you all feel pretty happy that it is over. It was a memorable occasion for the College and for the thousands who participated in the celebration.

It was a never-to-be-forgotten occasion, from which one brought away not only memories of beautiful sights and sounds and of inspiring words, but also an increased pride in women's achievements and opportunities and an enlarged sense of responsibility to help make the present and the future worthy of the past. All who had a part in planning and carrying out the countless details, not only of the program, but also for the comfort and pleasure of the guests, are to be congratulated upon a faultless accomplishment.

[From an alumna]

I wish I could find language sufficiently superlative to express my admiration for the celebration. The beauty, dignity and interest of the various ceremonies were matched by the efficiency and graciousness of the management. Any institution anywhere could be proud of that performance.

"I should like to pay tribute," said Miss Barbour in closing her report to the Centennial Committee, "to the never-to-be-forgotten co-operation of faculty, students, and alumnae, who worked together in harmony towards those days of commemoration. It was all heavy extracurricular work, and the spirit with which it was done was in itself a rich gift to the College."

President Woolley says: "It is not possible even to call the roll of the individuals who made the Centenary the success that it was, but there is one person who must be named. The importance of a coordinator was realized, one whose office would be a clearing house for all the ideas that might be evolved and all the plans that might be presented; an executive with a gift for details without losing the broader vision. That person was found in Marion Barbour, Mount Holyoke 1920, who with her assistants more than justified the confidence that was placed in them.

PUBLICITY

Publicity, ably handled by the College Press Bureau, was one of the most comprehensive tasks involved in the Centennial, including not only the reporting of the celebration itself, but a long advance program.

During the year 1936-37, public interest in the College was maintained by regular news releases, increasing in frequency as May approached, by magazine articles, photographs, and feature stories, as well as by a Centennial Series of radio programs broadcast by Station WSPR, Springfield, and the Colonial Network.

PRESS REPORTS. The Centenary Days were covered by the leading New York and Boston papers, by all the Springfield, Holyoke, and Hartford papers, and others, as well as by three wire services. *The New York Times* and *Herald-Tribune* and the *Christian Science Monitor* sent to the campus well-known feature writers. For the first time in the history of the College, wirephotos were sent directly from the Press Bureau to newspaper offices in all corners of the United States.

Perhaps the most complete record in both picture and story form was that contained in the two magazine-size supplements issued by the *Holyoke Transcript-Telegram*, featuring, as well as the days' events, a mass of historical material and countless pictures both historical and current.

RADIO. Through the courtesy of the National Broadcasting Company, the Columbia Broadcasting System, the World Wide Broadcasting Foundation, Station WSPR, and the Colonial Network, the celebrations were reported by radio to the world at large. Two coast-to-coast broadcasts, several programs heard along the Eastern seaboard, and complete short-wave broadcasts of the various events carried the voices of the principal speakers and of the student choirs to the many friends of the College unable to be present, and to many groups of alumnae who gathered together on May seventh and eighth to be present in spirit in South Hadley. Undoubtedly the most impressive broadcast was that of the conferring of honorary degrees, carried by the red network of NBC and by short-wave station WIXAL. Another effective program was the half hour of music by the combined choirs, presented direct from Mary Lyon Chapel over a coast-to-coast Columbia network. During a six-minute broadcast from the office of the Academic Dean, Miss Allyn and President Reinhardt of Mills College spoke briefly. The Serenade and Canoe Pageant, broadcast from two points on the lake shore by Stations WBZ and WBZA, with a running description by a commentator, made a novel program.

MOVING PICTURES. Moving-picture cameras made a record in color of the whole celebration, these films to be available in the Alumnae Office for loan to alumnae clubs and other groups.

FUND RAISING AND CENTENNIAL GIFTS

Certain policies with regard to Centennial fund raising were determined in December 1934—that the Office of the Field Secretary should be the central fund-raising organization, working with a Central Fund-Raising Committee of trustees, faculty, administrative officers, and alumnae; that all gifts received during the fiscal years 1935–36 and 1936–37 should be credited as Centennial gifts; and perhaps most important that appeals should not be made on the basis of definitely announced campaign goals.

There had been in existence for some time a clear outline of college needs which gave first place, on the academic side, to endowment for faculty salaries and emphasized the need of a large increase in scholarship funds. The building needs listed had been met in part before the academic year 1935–36 by the erection of the addition to the Library and a physics wing as the beginning of the Physics-Chemistry Building. Other buildings needed are a Gymnasium and Swimming Pool, for which the students and others are persistently accumulating money in small sums, a Recitation Building, and a museum wing for Dwight Art Memorial. The need for maintenance funds for both academic buildings and residence halls is acute.

Among the Centennial gifts is one building with a fund for its maintenance, the Abbey Chapel, named by the donor, Mrs. Emily F. Abbey Gill, of Springfield, Massachusetts, in memory of her late husband, Mr. Charles Clinton Abbey. Its corner stone was laid on Baccalaureate Sunday 1937. Approximately $400,000 has been promised as a bequest to be used probably for the completion of the Physics-Chemistry Building.

The alumnae were reached individually through the Alumnae Fund Committee of the Alumnae Association, working with the Alumnae Office and the Field Secretary's Office. The Alumnae Fund is a well-established institution which receives the annual contributions of alumnae. For the two years 1935–1937 these were counted as Centennial Gifts and a large proportion turned into the Mary E. Woolley Fund, the special project of this time. Among its activities the Alumnae Fund Committee presented to each alumna a series of folders and cards imaginatively conceived to foster a sense of unity and loyalty and to make the sharing in Centennial gifts a special privilege.

Classes being the normal unit of alumnae organization, each class had an agent to help with the follow-up in gathering the funds. There is an honor roll of one hundred and twenty-five alumnae who gave $50 or more in one of the two Centennial Years. It is a tradition that certain reunion classes make special gifts. At the one hundredth commencement the Class of 1887 gave $6,000 for a scholarship fund for a student in American history; the Class of 1912, $5,000 for a 1912 memorial scholarship fund; the Class of 1927, $1,965 for the Mary E. Woolley Fund; the Class of 1935, $578 for the Mary E. Woolley Fund. The pledge of Dr. Mary P. Dole of the Class of 1886, for a fellowship fund for a medical student, amounts to $5,000, the proceeds of her own hand-weaving.

Alumnae clubs, although their members belong primarily to classes, have their enthusiasm sustained by more frequent personal contacts and naturally make gifts as clubs. There were fifty-three memorial gifts made in honor of individual alumnae, ranging from the classes of 1838 to 1935. Some of the donors were relatives, some were alumnae friends, not relatives. The total of alumnae Centennial gifts and pledges is $200,812.

The Field Secretary's Office was quietly and constantly at work with the Central Fund-Raising Committee bringing special opportunities to the attention of friends and potential friends. One loyal friend of Miss Woolley and the College, Dr. John H. Finley, headed a Committee to invite non-alumnae friends to contribute to the Mary E. Woolley Fund for salary endowment. The total amount received and pledged from alumnae and others friends for this fund is $90,723.

There was sentiment based on close historic relationship in the birthday gifts from Wheaton, Lake Erie, and Wellesley Colleges.

A complete list of Centennial donors will be inscribed in a book to be bound in leather and deposited in the Treasure Room of the Library.

TOTAL CENTENNIAL GIFTS IN MONEY RECEIVED BY THE COLLEGE

For Special Purpose Funds	$38,289.43
For Building Funds	516,214.52
For Endowment Funds	282,507.77
For Conditional Gifts	40,750.00
For Unrestricted Purposes	10,353.00
For Miscellaneous Purposes	32,877.66
Total gifts of two years	$920,992.38

CENTENNIAL PUBLICATIONS

The time was ripe for a history of the Seminary and College against the background of New England social history. An experienced historian having a grasp of intellectual movements in the nineteenth and twentieth centuries in our country was sought to present Mount Holyoke in its historic setting. Such a one, Arthur C. Cole, Ph.D., Dean of the Graduate School of Western Reserve University, having access to hitherto unused source materials in our archives, is writing a detailed *History of Mount Holyoke College* as an organic part of the general history of education.

On a New England Campus, by a well-known and much-loved essayist, Frances Lester Warner, Litt.D., of the Class of 1911, is a book of essays filled with delightful reminiscences of Mount Holyoke personalities and incidents, both humorous and serious, written chiefly from twentieth-century memories of the author and of many other lovers of Mount Holyoke tradition. *Seminary Militant, an account of the missionary movement at Mount Holyoke Seminary and College*, by Louise Porter Thomas, Class of 1934, has been published by the English Department. It is a sympathetic interpretation of student response, beginning under Mary Lyon's guidance, to a great movement in the Protestant church which appealed to the heroic qualities inherent in human nature. A second volume of *Mount Holyoke College Verse*, comprising poems by fifty students from 1927 to 1937, has been edited by Ada L. F. Snell, Ph.D., Chairman of the Department of English, and published by the Oxford Press.

Other publications of significance include: The *One Hundred Year Biographical Directory of Mount Holyoke College*, 1837–1937, a detailed record of the sixteen thousand six hundred and twenty alumnae of the hundred years; *Register of the Faculty, Mount Holyoke College, 1936–1937*, giving in detail the training, experience and achievements of present faculty members; the Centennial Anthem, *Lord Thou Hast Been Our Dwelling Place*, composed by the College organist, Clara B. Tillinghast, M.A., Mount Holyoke 1902, privately printed; *Mount Holyoke College Choral Series*, works of great masters edited for women's voices by Miss Tillinghast, in course of publication by M. Witmark and Sons, New York; the catalogue of *An Exhibition of One Hundred American First Editions Paralleling the History of Mount Holyoke College* (See page 62); and the present volume, published as a record for participants and for present and future readers interested in Mount Holyoke College. A message from the Alumnae Club of Japan says that for its Centennial gift the group plans to secure the publication of some sketch of the life of Mary Lyon in Japanese.

A full-length documented biography of Mary Lyon under the title *Miss Lyon of Mount Holyoke* is in course of preparation by Sydney R. McLean, Ph.D., Assistant Professor of English at Mount Holyoke, and a graduate of the Class of 1922. Another alumna and an experienced writer, Marion F. Lansing, M.A., of the Class of 1903, is about to publish a book entitled *Mary Lyon through her Letters*. Both of these are unofficial publications.

Beginning in November 1936, four issues of the *Mount Holyoke Alumnae Quarterly* carried carefully planned and prepared Centennial material to its three thousand and more readers. The articles were written by members of the faculty and alumnae and included editorials, accounts of special phases of Mount Holyoke history, letters and reminiscences and photographs of the early and later days. The May issue with a specially designed blue and gold cover and an excellent reproduction of a drawing of the Seminary Building by an unknown artist of 1844 as its frontispiece was sent to ten thousand alumnae as the Centenary Edition. The August issue was no less special, however, and with pages of reports and photographs recaptured in generous measure the life and color of the Centenary Days.

Mention should also be made of student enterprises: historical articles in the *News*, the *Monthly*, and the *Llamarada;* histories of student organizations based on the Archives and College History Collections of the Library; and a gay series of colored bookmarks, bearing casual little drawings and brief "thumb-nail sketches" of important figures in college history, distributed as surprises from time to time at dormitory dinner tables.

CENTENNIAL ARCHIVES COMMITTEE. All of these publications and other papers concerned with the Centenary, including such minor items as invitations, programs, tickets, and announcements, also press reports, current magazine articles, and College views have been assembled for preservation and use in one unified collection in the Library. In addition to the

Centennial material the collection includes reports and documents constituting a survey of the College, its organization—trustees, administrative officers, faculty—the Community Government and student organizations, the Alumnae Association and Alumnae Clubs. Academic standards and methods are revealed by exhibits and by histories of departments of instruction. The physical plant and the functions of different buildings are included in the survey. The historically minded Archives Committee has made this a useful collection of source material on the history of Mount Holyoke College.

THE TRUSTEES AND FACULTY OF
AMHERST COLLEGE
TO THE TRUSTEES AND FACULTY OF
MOUNT HOLYOKE COLLEGE

Greeting:

Amherst College, rejoicing in many happy associations with South Hadley from the time of the establishment there of the first institution for the higher education of women, sends its congratulations to Mount Holyoke College on the one hundredth anniversary of the founding by Mary Lyon of Mount Holyoke Seminary.

Gladly availing themselves of the invitation to be represented at the Centenary exercises on May the seventh and eighth, nineteen hundred and thirty-seven, the Trustees and Faculty of Amherst College have appointed Stanley King, LL.D., President of the College, as their delegate, and have charged him to convey their felicitations and their hope that Amherst and Mount Holyoke, sprung from the same soil and sharing the same skyline, may flourish in neighborly helpfulness, an inspiration each to each, for centuries to come.

Given at Amherst, Massachusetts, on the seventeenth day of April, in the year of Our Lord the nineteen hundred and thirty-seventh, and of Amherst College the one hundred and sixteenth.

C. Scott Porter, Dean	Cornelius H. Patton
Wm. J. Newlin, Sec'y	Alfred E. Stearns
George F. Whicher	Lucius R. Eastman
For the Faculty	*For the Trustees*

THE CARNEGIE FOUNDATION
FOR THE ADVANCEMENT OF TEACHING

Thanks in large part to the steadfast enthusiasm of Mary Lyon, Mount Holyoke Seminary took its place among pioneering institutions for the development of "enlightened, useful women." For a century Mount Holyoke has offered her students the best that is known in thought in the world.

The Carnegie Foundation for the Advancement of Teaching felicitates Mount Holyoke College upon the occasion of this centenary celebration and offers its best wishes for a fruitful and happy future.

March the nineteenth
Nineteen hundred and thirty-seven

THE UNIVERSITY OF CHICAGO

TO THE TRUSTEES AND THE FACULTY OF MOUNT HOLYOKE COLLEGE

GREETING

The University of Chicago
has delegated

Charles Whitney Gilkey, A.M., D.D.
Professor of Preaching and
Dean of University Chapel
in The University of Chicago

Shailer Mathews, A.M., D.D., LL.D.
Professor Emeritus of Historical Theology and
Dean Emeritus of the Divinity School
in The University of Chicago

Marion Talbot, A.M., LL.D.
Professor Emeritus of Household Administration
in The University of Chicago

as its representatives at the
Centenary Celebration
of the Founding of the College

The University welcomes the opportunity heartily to congratulate Mount Holyoke College upon its leadership in the field of higher education for women, and to express the hope that its service may continue to be of ever increasing distinction.

Robert Maynard Hutchins
President

VNIVERSITAS COLVMBIAE
IN VRBE NOVO EBORACO SITA
COLLEGIO MONTIS HOLYOKENSIS
S.P.D.

Litteras vestras, viri clarissimi, laeto animo perlegimus in quibus memoriam Academiae vestrae abhinc annos iam centum conditae mox recognituri nos quoque laetitiae istius et testes et participes esse tam comiter voluistis. Quibus feriis ut tamquam praesentes frueremur, quam statim libenter, quippe qui vobiscum et scientiarum studiis et omnibus moribus pacis amicitiaeque consociati essemus, legatum ad vos mittere decrevimus.

Gaudemus quod Academia vestra per hos annos felices in bonis artibus et docendis et promovendis tanta cum laude versata est. Gaudemus quod ex ista sede amplissima doctrinarum tot ingeniosae ad munera vitae suscipienda eo consilio prodierunt ut ingenuas illas disseminarent artes quae ad salutem et concordiam totius generis humani pertinerent. Nam ex illis demum studiis effloruit haec libertas cum mentis tum rei publicae qua communiter vobiscum iam diu utimur. Hanc quidem libertatem utinam indagatio veri per quam solam intellegi potest qualis intercedat necessitudo inter hominem ipsum et universam rerum naturam magis magisque confirmet atque tueatur.

Vestrae igitur voluntati obsecuti, unam e nostro doctorum coetu,

Virginia Crocheron Gildersleeve, Ph.D., Litt.D., LL.D., feminam et ipsam eruditissimam et ad hoc munus praecipue idoneam ad vos legavimus quae nostrum omnium nomine vobis gratularetur et in posterum omnia fausta feliciaque exoptaret.

Valete

Nicholas Murray Butler

Praeses

Dabamus Novi Eboraci
 Kalendis Maiis
  Anno Salutis MCMXXXVII

THE TRUSTEES AND FACULTIES OF
CORNELL UNIVERSITY
TO THE TRUSTEES AND THE FACULTY OF
MOUNT HOLYOKE COLLEGE
GREETING:

Your gracious invitation to be present at the Centenary Celebration of the Founding of Mount Holyoke College, which you are to hold at South Hadley on the Seventh and Eighth of May, Nineteen Hundred and Thirty-Seven, is accepted with pleasure.

We welcome this opportunity of joining in the tribute of praise which institutions of learning pay to the wisdom and the courage of your Founder. What she achieved has become so much more than the creation of a single college that the very freedom of liberal education today is indebted to the example of Mount Holyoke. Merely as the prototype of the college for women her foundation would be memorable, but what you celebrate is greater even than that. Mount Holyoke's century has seen colleges and universities everywhere admitting women to the full enjoyment of educational privileges, denied them in Mary Lyon's day by a prejudice which she challenged and dispelled. That century has seen educated women proving their competence as workers in scholarship and creative science, in the public service, and in the learned professions. Cornell University shares in your rejoicing the more eagerly because its own graduates include women whose trained abilities are thus exercised.

We give to Mary Merritt Crawford, Doctor of Medicine, one of our graduates and a member of our Board of Trustees, commission as our Delegate to attend your Centenary Celebration and to bring you our hearty felicitations and good wishes.

Given at Ithaca, New York, April the Fifteenth, Nineteen Hundred and Thirty-Seven.

Livingston Farrand
President

THE TRUSTEES AND THE FACULTY OF GOUCHER COLLEGE TO THE TRUSTEES AND THE FACULTY OF MOUNT HOLYOKE COLLEGE, GREETING:

To Mount Holyoke College celebrating the centenary of its foundation Goucher College presents congratulations and thanks for its inspiring devotion to the education of women. During a hundred years Mount Holyoke College, ever adjusting to new conditions and ever loyal to the high ideals of Mary Lyon, has been a Fostering Mother not only to her own daughters but to countless others. "She is clothed with strength and dignity and she laughs at the days to come." May the future afford even greater cause for congratulations.

Given at Goucher College, in the City of Baltimore and the State of Maryland, on the fifth day of May, in the year of Our Lord the nineteen hundred and thirty-seventh, and of Goucher College the fifty-second.

David Allan Robertson
President

THE PRESIDENT AND FELLOWS OF
HARVARD COLLEGE
TO THE PRESIDENT AND BOARD OF TRUSTEES
OF MOUNT HOLYOKE COLLEGE
GREETING:

THE College of JOHN HARVARD salutes the College of MARY LYON on its Hundredth Birthday. An institution which pointed the way to the higher education of women has a special right to the veneration which age inspires; for it can claim not only priority in age but also the honor reserved for the makers of a great tradition. A true seminary it was, not only in the sense which the era of its foundation frequently applied to all institutions of learning, but also as a seed-plot where the ideals and hopes and labors of a devoted founder took root and flowered in the College of today, disseminating their fruitage in the lives of thousands of your daughters; flowered, too, in scores of other colleges which can trace their inspiration to the faith and daring of MARY LYON. Like Sir Walter Mildmay, founder of John Harvard's College of Emmanuel, she might have said, "I have set an Acorn, which when it becomes an Oak, God alone knows what will be the fruit thereof."

GOD alone knew; for the founder of MOUNT HOLYOKE could not have dreamt of the great number and diversity of careers that the coming century would open to women—careers for which higher education would be a prerequisite. To say this is not quite to say that she built more wisely than she knew; for if teaching then seemed likely to be preëminently the career for educated women, she saw further than other leaders of her time into the future of that profession. Moreover, in so doing, she did not narrow her conception of the purpose of liberal education. She did not see in the career of the teacher the sole, or even the main, justification of higher education. No false antithesis between training for a profession and training for life was in her mind. It was in order that women as such, women as members of the community, women as builders and protectors of family life, should be equal to the highest intellectual and spiritual demands of these relationships and responsibilities, and equipped for the fullest realization of their individual capacities, that Mary Lyon labored with indomitable courage and patience to establish this College. When, with the social and economic changes the century was soon to bring, the opportunities and privileges of women were enlarged, no new principle had to be invoked to justify the opening to them of all the resources of liberal education. The demand for it was vastly multiplied, but the reason for it had been laid down when MOUNT HOLYOKE was founded.

IT is a happy circumstance that the Centennial of one of the first institutions for the higher education of women in the United States so nearly coincides with the third centennial of collegiate education in this country. For it unites us all at this time in reverence to the faith and zeal of the founders and in the re-dedication of all colleges and universities to their high and indispensable function in our American democracy. Never has it been more essential that the lamp of learning should be fed and that its light should be held aloft than in these troubled times.

OF the light here lit by your sainted founder and zealously tended by her successors it may be said, in the words of Governor Bradford, " . . . as one small candle may light a thousand, so the light here kindled hath shone to many, yea in some sort to our whole nation; let the glorious name of Jehova have all the praise!"

WE beg you to accept the hearty congratulations of Harvard University upon the completion of your first century and our fevent hopes for your happiness and prosperity in all the centuries to come.

Given at Cambridge, Massachusetts, this first day of May in the Year of Our Lord the one thousand nine hundred and thirty-seventh and of Harvard College the three hundred and first.

For the PRESIDENT AND FELLOWS OF HARVARD COLLEGE.

Jerome D. Greene, *Secretary to the Corporation*

McMASTER UNIVERSITY
HAMILTON, ONTARIO

TO THE TRUSTEES AND THE FACULTY
MOUNT HOLYOKE COLLEGE
SOUTH HADLEY, MASSACHUSETTS, U.S.A.

McMaster University appreciates the honour of your kind invitation to be represented at the Centenary Celebration, to be held on the seventh and eighth days of May. We share your pride in the courage and vision of Mary Lyon and her colleagues and successors in the foundation and conduct of Mount Holyoke Female Seminary, and in the growth of that seminary to become Mount Holyoke College in 1888. We are conscious of the contribution made by your institution, not only through its members, but through the example of its work which has led to the foundation of similar schools of higher learning for young women in your own and other lands. To have completed a century of existence is in itself a notable achievement: to have completed it with such success, such enlargement and such enjoyment of public and academic goodwill is an inspiration not only to yourselves but to all interested with you in the advancement of learning, the wholesome discipline of the mind, and the provision of opportunities for youth to find its way in succeeding generations. Please accept our hearty congratulations upon your achievements and upon the possession of so great a tradition, and our sincere hope for your continuance and growth in success and usefulness.

To represent us at your celebration we have appointed the Reverend George Arthur Clarke, a graduate of this University, who is the minister of the First Baptist Church of Malden, Massachusetts.

Yours cordially,
Howard P. Whidden
Chancellor

April 26th, 1937

THE CHANCELLOR, PRINCIPAL, GOVERNORS, AND
FELLOWS OF McGILL UNIVERSITY TO THE TRUS-
TEES AND FACULTY OF MOUNT HOLYOKE COLLEGE
UPON THE OCCASION OF THE CENTENARY OF ITS
FOUNDING, GREETING:

McGill University takes with especial pleasure this opportunity of adding its voice to the chorus of congratulations that will rightly acclaim a hundred years of distinguished effort and achievement.

To this end Arthur Eustace Morgan, Principal and Vice-Chancellor of the University, has been appointed to express to you good wishes and the lively hope that Mount Holyoke College may continue long to flourish like a palm tree beside cool waters and to produce daughters as corner stones polished after the similitude of a palace.

E. W. Beatty
Chancellor

T. H. Matthews
Registrar

A. E. Morgan
Principal

Given in Montreal under the seal of the University this third day of May in the year one thousand nine hundred and thirty-seven.

THE CHANCELLOR, COUNCIL, AND FACULTY OF NEW YORK UNIVERSITY
TO THE PRESIDENT, TRUSTEES, AND FACULTY OF MOUNT HOLYOKE COLLEGE

Greeting:

We are gratified to participate in the expression of felicitation and goodwill from the academic fraternity at large to Mount Holyoke College on the occasion of the celebration of the institution's centenary. We rejoice with the great company of those identified with the College at its distinguished history, present eminence, and promising future, which amply justify this celebration. We trust that the first century of notable achievements soon to be commemorated may in centuries to come be reckoned as a glorious prelude to the greater growth in prosperity and public usefulness of Mount Holyoke College that is now so happily presaged.

Respectfully,

Harold O. Voorhis   Harry Woodburn Chase
Secretary   *Chancellor of New York University*

Dated May 1, 1937
in the City of New York

RANDOLPH-MACON WOMAN'S COLLEGE

January 19, 1937

President Mary E. Woolley,
Mount Holyoke College,
South Hadley, Massachusetts.

My dear President Woolley:

When the rigours of the winter season in bleak New England shall be well overpast, Randolph-Macon Woman's College, constantly enjoying the balmy clime of the ancient Commonwealth of Virginia, will delight to join in the celebration of the one hundredth birthday of her highly esteemed and greatly beloved sister, Mount Holyoke, and will send her President from her seat on the banks of the lordly James under the very shadow of the Blue Ridge to bear her greetings in person.

Godspeed Mount Holyoke, and God bless her President!

Sincerely yours,
Theodore H. Jack
President

VASSAR COLLEGE

On the occasion of the hundredth anniversary of the founding of Mount Holyoke College, Vassar College presents greetings, and congratulates her sister college for the great service rendered in the promotion of education in America.

Henry Noble MacCracken
President

May the seventh
Nineteen hundred and thirty-seven

TO THE TRUSTEES AND THE FACULTY OF
MOUNT HOLYOKE COLLEGE
GREETINGS

The Chancellor, the President, the Board of Governors, the Senate and the Faculties of the University of Western Ontario send their congratulations to Mount Holyoke College on the occasion of the celebration of her centenary.

From her founding Mount Holyoke College has sent forth women whose devotion to scholarship has borne eloquent testimony to the principles of sound education inculcated by their Alma Mater. We send our felicitations fully confident that she will continue her loyal adherence to the high ideals of learning which have so gloriously inspired her in the past.

Given at London, Ontario, April seventh, nineteen hundred and thirty-seven.

W. Sherwood Fox
President and Vice-Chancellor

K. P. R. Neville
Registrar

THE WOMEN'S CHRISTIAN COLLEGE

The Women's Christian College, Madras, South India, sends filial and grateful greetings to Mount Holyoke College on the happy occasion which marks the attainment of a hundred years of illustrious life. It is more than twenty years now since Mount Holyoke, the oldest and most famous of Women's Colleges in the world, first expressed a kindly interest in the venture of starting a women's college of similar ideals and principles in the South of India, and since that time her generous and manifold kindness to her young and struggling sister college has been unfailing. Our Vice-Principal, and the heads of two of our teaching departments are alumnae of Mount Holyoke, and have made and are making constructive and formative contributions of the highest order to our still developing system. Others of the Faculty of Mount Holyoke have strengthened and encouraged us by working on our Staff for a year or two years, and we hope that such visits may be frequent. At this very moment we are thinking with mingled gratitude and sorrow of Dr. Stokey who after a second visit to enrich our Botany Department has just left us for her return journey to her work in Mount Holyoke. Every year we receive from the Alumnae Chest help which has been of the greatest value to us in our sadly straitened circumstances. Alumnae of ours have been most kindly welcomed at Mount Holyoke and have come back greatly enriched in mind and spirit. We view our connection with this our Sister College with great pride and gratitude, and we send our loving congratulations with the hope that we may in some degree render to South India the service which Mount Holyoke has rendered to the national life of America.

For the Council
Eleanor McDougall
Principal

TRIBUTES TO PRESIDENT WOOLLEY

Excerpts from a few of the personal tributes which the editor persuaded Miss Woolley to let her choose for this book.

[From the President of the British Federation of University Women.]

. . . Dr. Melville is especially sorry that she will miss the opportunity of meeting once again the distinguished President of the College, Miss Mary Woolley, whose acquaintance she first made at St. Andrews University, Scotland, in the year of Miss Woolley's appointment to Mount Holyoke Presidency. From that time, it has been a matter of great personal interest to hear the name of Mount Holyoke College because of European reputation, through the eminence of its Alumnae but, above all, through its association with the name of President Mary Woolley.

Dr. Frances Melville offers her hearty congratulations to the College on the attainment of its Hundredth Year and its unique position as the oldest Woman's College in the World.

[From Graduates under Miss Woolley's Administration]

In the great company of Mount Holyoke women around the world I am sending my thoughts back to South Hadley these days. For those of us who cannot attend the Centenary festivities, the celebration is characterized by a process of soul searching to make vivid the values for which Mount Holyoke stands and consciously to relate one's current experience to them. The gathering up of the heritage of one hundred years must engender a quickening of life and a deepening of courage to carry forward the work begun by Mary Lyon.

For me, as for thousands of graduates, this occasion brings a new realization of the ways in which you have embodied the Mount Holyoke ideal. Because you put that ideal into words for me, on many public and private occasions, and also, and more especially, because you have stood to me for the very quality of life to which you urged my allegiance, I cannot think of my Mount Holyoke heritage apart from you.

In token of a gratitude which cannot be adequately expressed in words, but is constantly acknowledged in my daily living, I send my affectionate greetings to you on Mount Holyoke's One Hundredth Anniversary.

I cannot forego the privilege of telling you how very happy we all were in the great celebration—Mount Holyoke's day of glory—last week! We did not have an opportunity of grasping your hand and speaking to you face to face—and telling you how very, very deeply we all feel about your thirty-seven years of devoted and remarkable leadership of our College! We will ever hold it all in deep and affectionate remembrance. You have been privileged to build yourself into the lives of so many, many young women, and we know that you have been an increasing inspiration to thousands of us who sat under your leadership, or have felt your influence in the years since our immediate college days.

The College, so beautiful and so complete and so alluring in its dignity and beauty as we saw it last week, is a monument to your splendid vision and sacrificial labors.

It truly must be a source of deepest satisfaction to you that you have wrought so nobly, and that you have had the *opportunity* to serve your generation so worthily and well. To say that we are all very proud of and *grateful* for your achievement is to be trite, were it not that it is so *true* and *unanimous*.

To all of us who have had the privilege of being in college while you were its President, Mount Holyoke and Miss Woolley seem to stand for the same thing. Whether we realize it or not, your ideals which you so thoroughly, but so quietly emphasized, govern our behavior. Frances Warner's chapter on Miss Woolley brought back even your voice. I wonder, do you still say in Vespers and in morning chapel, "The Lord bless all those who are dear to us and keep us all in Thy care, constantly lifting our hearts unto Thee for guidance"? I say it every day and *never* without hearing your voice. That is but one example of the many ways in which you have made us all yours—proud daughters of Mount Holyoke and Miss Woolley.

You have given us an example of what a world citizen ought to be. We cannot all hold important positions but we can all put into our jobs the qualities of your spirit: courage, idealism, integrity and love.

. . . Yet these accomplishments, remarkable as they are, seem not as great to me as the fact that you have inspired thousands of us with the ideals for our daily living.

May I add a bit to the festivity of your party for it is your party. You, only second to Mary Lyon herself, have made Mount Holyoke what it is today and we are so happy to be able to share the great day with you.

This must be a very glorious time for you. And I am sure that for those of us who cannot come as well as for those who will be in South Hadley you will be the living centre of this great celebration. There must be many thousands who are grateful to you today and today you must have a great many memories of the years past.

But better than all the machinery of the celebration was the abiding spirit one felt of gratitude for the accomplishments of the past one hundred years. The tributes to the part you have played in the history of Mount Holyoke College were echoed by the thousands of your students who heard them.

[From graduates previous to Miss Woolley's Administration].

Before I return home from this great Centenary celebration, I want to tell you what a thrill I have had in being in South Hadley and in seeing you receive the honor and the praise from all sides that you so richly deserve. It really seemed like a crowning event for you for the great work you have done for more than a third of the century.

It was most thrilling and inspiring to hear and see such a galaxy of brilliant and able women and to have them spread before us the truly marvellous achievements of women in all lines. I shall live the rest of my life in the warm glow of that picture.

We have only to glance about us to see the material gains that have been achieved during your administration. For these we thank you, but far more we take pride in the way you have upheld the high ideals of Mount Holyoke for sound scholarship, righteousness, and unselfish service for mankind.

[From Mount Holyoke Trustees]

What an outstanding success was yesterday—*your* day—at our Mount Holyoke. Everything moved off with precision and perfection, and we want to extend our warmest congratulations to you, and your gallant attendants, who so devotedly and skillfully cared for the comfort and pleasure of every visitor. . . . As for yourself and the masterly way in which you carried off the big morning program, you never appeared to better advantage. Those personal citations to the Honorable Degree recipients were clever, dramatic and wonderful.

I am writing now to tell you how deeply impressed I was by the dignity of the entire performance and how cordially I echoed the many statements of congratulation which the various speakers made to you personally.

I trust the ordeal of the two days has not tired you unduly. The College has received universal praise for the excellent management of the ceremonies and I am sure that you share with all of us connected with the College a feeling of deep gratification that the celebration of our hundredth birthday has been so successful.

[From Representatives of Universities and Colleges]

I am writing to express to you my sincere appreciation of the opportunity which was offered to me to participate in the Centenary Ceremonies at Mount Holyoke College. I enjoyed very much the exercises on Saturday morning. They were delightfully appropriate to the occasion. Personally, I was very much impressed by the addresses and by the ceremony by which the honorary degrees were conferred.

I join with all others who were present in deep appreciation of the tributes which were paid to you, to your distinguished leadership at Mount Holyoke College, to your significant contributions to the field of education and to your important place in the world of affairs.

I cannot let this significant event pass without sending to you a personal word of congratulation upon your share in making the one hundred years of Mount Holyoke's life so distinguished. I have long admired the dignity with which you have maintained the great traditions of the past and your leadership in meeting the new problems of the present time. Now that I have had a few years' experience as a college president, and know the difficulties of maintaining one's ideals in the face of compromising situations that seem inevitable in these changing times, I have a greater admiration for such distinguished leadership as you have given.

I did not have opportunity to speak to you during my visit at Mount Holyoke, but I want to write you a word of appreciation for all that you have meant to the world. It was very gratifying to see the especially large representation of institutions at the Centennial exercises. I found that the general feeling was that such an outpouring was an expression of regard for you and what you have accomplished.

I know by experience that retirement does not mean inactivity, and I hope that your health will permit you to carry on some of those tasks which so much need your guidance and help.

May I also express personally my very great admiration for your splendid leadership, not only in the work of the College, but also in connection with so many important matters of public concern. I trust the years after your retirement, which I hope will be many, will bring to you great happiness and increasing satisfaction in what you have accomplished.

The achievements of Mount Holyoke College throughout a hundred years are so manifold and so remarkable that the nation takes pride in them.

APPENDIX

PROGRAMS

MUSIC BY THE CHOIRS

A program of music by the combined College Choirs of three hundred voices given in Mary Lyon Chapel on the seventh and eighth of May at three o'clock.

Dr. William Churchill Hammond, *Director*
Ruth Douglass, *Associate Conductor and Soloist*
Clara Tillinghast, *Organist*
Viva Faye Richardson, *Pianist*

Festival Anthem: I Beheld and Lo......................*Clara Tillinghast*
(Composed for Founder's Day 1930)

Blessed Jesu, Fount of Mercy—from "Stabat Mater"..............*Dvorak*
Jubilate, Amen...*Bruch*
Soprano solo and chorus

May No Rash Intruder—from "Solomon".......................*Handel*
(The above three selections are arranged and edited by Clara Tillinghast)

Quintet, E Flat Major.....................................*Beethoven*
Allegro ma non troppo   Andante cantabile
(Arranged for piano and organ)

Cantata, Saint Mary Magdalene..............................*d'Indy*
Soprano solo and chorus

Anthem composed for the Centenary Celebration..............*Tillinghast*

Lord, Thou hast been our dwelling-place in all generations.
Before the mountains were brought forth, or ever the earth and the world
were made,
Thou art God from everlasting, world without end.
For a thousand years in Thy sight are but as yesterday when it is past,
and as a watch in the night.
O teach us to number our days, that we may apply our hearts unto wis-
dom.

Show Thy servants Thy work and their children Thy glory,
That our daughters may be as corner-stones polished after the similitude
    of a palace.[1]
A virtuous woman is far above rubies. Give her of the fruit of her hands,
    and let her own works praise her in the gates.[2]
And the glorious majesty of the Lord our God be upon us, and establish
    Thou the work of our hands upon us.

O God, our help in ages past,
Our hope for years to come,
Be Thou our guard while life shall last,
And our eternal home. Amen.

        Psalm 90: 1, 2, 4, 12, 16, 17; Psalm 144: 12; Proverbs 31: 10, 31;
        Verse of St. Anne.

[1] Biblical reference on the Mount Holyoke College seal.
[2] Inscription on the monument of Mary Lyon, Founder of Mount Holyoke.

THE LABORATORY THEATRE
CENTENNIAL PRODUCTION
May 7 and 8, 1937 at 3 P.M.

This program is dedicated to

PRESIDENT MARY EMMA WOOLLEY

in honor of her distinguished service in the
education of women and in the cause
of world peace

THE VEST POCKET STANDBY

By ELEANORE PRICE '32

Presented by Introductory Laboratory Theatre, 1936–1937

PERSONS IN THE PLAY

Nurse...*Louise Rayner*
Marianne...*Ann Hebb*

Johnny . . . . *Emily Gifford*
General . . . . *Beatrice Milligan*
Colonel . . . . *Benita Beck*
Major . . . . *Marcia Kidder*
Captain . . . . *Pauline Dyer*
Lieutenant . . . . *Ruth Matthews*
Jack-in-the-Box . . . . *Eleanor Pitts*

Time: The Past?

Place: A Battle Front for Dolls

Director . . . . *Jeannette Marks*
Assistant Director . . . . *Dean N. Currie*
Coach . . . . *Louise Wallis*
'Script Heads . . . . { *Jeannette Marks*
                                                                  Lawrence B. Wallis
Business Manager . . . . *Lawrence B. Wallis*
Production Crews:
    Costumer . . . . *Louise Wallis*
        Assistants . . . . *Eleanor Bartlett, Sarah Johnston, Beverley White*
    Electrician . . . . *Jeannette Marks*
        Assistant . . . . *Dean N. Currie*
    Make-up Masters. *Annamarie Booz, Janie Clark, Mary Jane Purrington*
    Music . . . . *Margaret McKay Burgevin*
    Prompter . . . . *Lorraine Seaver*
    Property Master . . . . *Elsa Krause*
    Scene Designer . . . . *Dorothy Merriman '32*
    Sound Master . . . . *Elizabeth Cutter*
    Stage Manager . . . . *Elizabeth Gillilan*
        Assistants . . . . *Alice Austin, Barbara Baldwin,*
                                                            Dean Hoffman, Virginia Wilbur
    Technical Crew . . . . *Elizabeth Ochiltree, Evelyne Seibold*
                                                            Emily Thompson, Natalie Tucker
    Head Ushers . . . . *Dorothy Goldstein, Beverley White*
    Assistants . . . . *Mary Anderson, Mary Lou Baylies, Helen Brett,*
                                     Sara Gooding, Ruth Heller, Ciel Jablonower,
                        Muriel Kemble, Eleanor MacElwee, Nessie MacQuillan,
                            Alice Nestler, Ruth Niceswanger, Margaret Peck,
                            Doris Pullman, Catharine Rand, Carol Stillwell,
                        Jean Tinkham, Mary Elizabeth White, Ruth Willan

CENTENARY EXHIBITION

Works of Art by Mount Holyoke Alumnae and Members of the Faculty. An Exhibition Sponsored by the Department of Art, the Hollingsworth Fund, and the Mount Holyoke Friends of Art, May 7 through June 18, Dwight Art Memorial.

EDITH A. ABBOTT, 1904   *Rockport, Mass.*

    From a New England Garden   Oil
    Sunshine and Shadow, Honolulu   Oil

AMY BRIGGS BALDWIN, 1920   *Tallahassee, Fla.*
    (*Mrs. Rollin S. Baldwin*)

    West Call Street   Gouache
    Pineapple   Oil
    Harbor of Corfu   Brush Drawing
    The Ghetto, Brusa   Brush Drawing
    Galata Tower   Woodblock
    Vefa Djami   Woodblock

E. FRANCES BOTSFORD, 1916   *New London, Conn.*

    Waterfront   Oil
    Thames River   Oil

CLARA T. CLEMENT, 1907   *Wellesley, Mass.*

    Rockport Wharf   Oil
    Rockport Scene   Water Color

JOSEPHINE G. COCHRANE, 1885   *Washington, D. C.*

    A Basque Balcony, St. Jean de Luz   Oil
    La Cimetière (Basque)   Oil
    L'Impasse, Bruges   Oil
    Quai de la Main d'Or, Bruges   Oil
    Sunset, Lake O'Hara   Oil
    Mt. Leffroy, Lake Louise   Oil

HELEN WIEAND COLE, 1906   *Nantucket, Mass.*
    (*Mrs. Samuel V. Cole*)

    A Summer Day *or* Nantucket Marshes   Oil
    Memory of a Sunset in Florida   Oil

MIRIAM W. COOK, 1933   *Scarsdale, N. Y.*

    Memorial Staircourt   Landscape Design
    Christ Church, Cambridge   Wash Drawing
        (Lent by Mrs. O. B. Fairbanks)
    A Sculptor's Studio   Landscape Design

HELEN E. FERNALD, 1914   *Orlando, Fla.*

    Windermere, Florida   Oil
    In the Berkshires   Oil
    Eastern Point, Gloucester, Massachusetts   Oil

FLORENCE FOSS, 1905   *South Hadley, Mass.*

    The Challenge   Aluminum Sculpture
    Humoresque   Aluminum Sculpture
    Cat at Ease   Aluminum Sculpture

PAMELIA JACOBS GIBB, 1932   *Belmont, Mass.*
    (*Mrs. John C. Gibb*)

    October Wedding   Costume Designs

MARGARET C. GRIGOR, 1934   *Bryn Mawr, Pa.*

    Portrait head of Orin Raphael   Plaster Sculpture
    Portrait relief of My Mother   Plaster Sculpture

RUTH MACKRILLE HAMMOND, 1915   *Brunswick, Me.*
    (*Mrs. Edward S. Hammond*)

    House of Tiberius, Rome   Water Color
    Appian Way   Water Color
    The Wishbone Tree, Florida   Water Color
    Casco Bay   Water Color

GEORGE HASKELL, Campus Employe   *South Hadley, Mass.*

    Evening Glow   Oil

MABEL L. HEDGE, 1909   *Deceased*

    Amalfi   Etching
    Medical Illustrations

ELIZABETH HENRICH, 1933   *Brookline, Mass.*

    Portrait of Negro Youth   Charcoal and White Chalk Drawing
    Portrait of a Young Girl   Charcoal and White Chalk Drawing
    Photographs of Medical Illustrations

PRUDENCE HERRICK, 1920   *New York, N. Y.*

    The Offering   Water Color
    Halebid Temple   Water Color
    Street Scene, Lahore   Print

EMILY L. HOFFMEIER, 1909   *West Chester, Pa.*

    Main Street, Nantucket   Oil
    Old South Wharf, Nantucket   Oil

GERTRUDE HERRICK HOWE, 1924   *Ardsley, N. Y.*
    (*Mrs. Arthur Howe*)

    Bananas   Water Color
    Cod Liver Oil   Water Color
    Splash!   Water Color

GERTRUDE S. HYDE, 1896   *South Hadley, Mass.*

    Fumiko   Oil
    Portuguese Woman—Study   Oil

ELISABETH AVERILL JACKSON, 1931   *Philadelphia, Pa.*
    (*Mrs. Elmore Jackson*)

    Outdoor Theatre   Architectural Drawing
    Backdrop for a Musical Revue   Pastel

EVIS TOWLE JENNINGS, 1933   *New Brunswick, N. J.*
    (*Mrs. Andrew B. Jennings*)

    Andrew Jennings   Plaster Sculpture
    Hazel Andresen   Plaster Sculpture
    Mary Anna Vail (Park)   Plaster Sculpture

BARBARA JOHNSON, 1935   *West Medford, Mass.*

    Landscape   Oil

DOROTHY KILTON, 1915   *Worcester, Mass.*

Abandoned Lime Kiln (Thomaston, Maine)   Water Color
Shore Shanty (Boothbay Harbor, Maine)   Water Color

HELEN McAUSLAN, 1917   *Westfield, N. J.*

Railroad Station   Oil
Cliffs on Powder River   Water Color

ENID ALLEN NASH, 1913   *South Norwalk, Conn.*
(*Mrs. Douglas E. Nash*)

House Where Mary Lyon Had Her First School   Oil
Bavarian Mountains   Oil

HELEN F. NEWTON, 1900   *Woodbridge, Conn.*

Tunnel Road, Santa Barbara   Oil
Cascades of Lupine   Oil
Spring Hillsides, Laguna Canyon   Oil
In the Fingers of the Fog   Oil

JANET ROBERTS, 1935   *New York, N. Y.*

Commercial Designs   Two-Color Lithographs

ELISABETH ROBINSON, 1928   *Syracuse, N. Y.*

Sheepshead Bay   Oil
Striving   Imitation Woodblock
Study   Pencil Drawing

HELEN V. RUNNETTE, 1909   *Salem, Mass.*

Spray   Oil
Hills   Oil
Stormy Day   Oil

ROGERS D. RUSK, Faculty   *South Hadley, Mass.*

Old Boston   Water Color

SARAH E. RUSK, Former Member of Faculty   *South Hadley, Mass.*
(*Mrs. Rogers D. Rusk*)

Early Autumn   Water Color

GRACE COOLEY SMILLIE, 1910   *Essex Fells, N. J.*
    (*Mrs. Ralph Smillie*)

    Bowl   Pottery
    Squirrel   Buff Clay Waxed
    Bowl   Pottery

HILDEGARDE SNOW, 1926   *Framingham, Mass.*

    Contemporary Bacchante   Pewter Sculpture
    Silence   Plaster Sculpture
    Liebestraum   Plaster Sculpture

NELLIE DODD SPEERS, 1912   *Montclair, N. J.*
    (*Mrs. James M. Speers*)

    Angel—Revelation 20: 1   Plaster Sculpture
    Head of Child—"Margie"   Plaster Sculpture
    Salutation to Light   Bronze Sculpture

JESSIE B. TREFETHEN, 1906   *Oberlin, Ohio*

    Deep Forest, Ontario   Water Color
    Little Harbor, Long Island, Maine   Water Color
    Todd's Head   Water Color
    November in Ohio   Water Color
    Severn River, Ohio   Water Color

JULIA M. WICKHAM, 1888   *Cutchogue, N. Y.*

    Peonies in Chinese Jar   Oil
    Street Scene, Cape Ann   Oil
    Sugar Loaf Mountain, Lake George   Oil

IRMA C. WIEAND, 1901   *Nantucket, Mass.*

    Koko Head, Honolulu   Oil
    Swiss Church   Oil

ANNA I. WOODBURY, 1911   *Worcester, Mass.*

    John Alden Family   Wood Carving
    Moving Day among the Blackfeet   Wood Carving
    The Myles Standish Family Car   Wood Carving

KATHERINE F. WORCESTER, 1903   *Burlington, Vt.*

    Landscape—Early Spring   Oil
    Interior   Oil
    Portrait "Now We are Six"   Oil

PROGRAM OF DEPARTMENTAL EXHIBITS

Mount Holyoke College cordially invites its Centenary guests to inspect its classrooms, libraries, studios, and laboratories. For one hundred years, as seminary and college, Mount Holyoke has sought to give to women opportunities for liberal education equal to those offered to men. The growth and expansion as well as the present scope of its educational program are sketched in the exhibits here presented.

ANTHROPOLOGY

Cornelia Clapp Laboratory: Museum of Prehistory, Second Floor, West End

Archaeological specimens from the stone ages of Europe and America, with comparative material from other parts of the world. Casts representing certain prehistoric races.

ART AND ARCHAEOLOGY

Dwight Art Memorial

Special Centenary exhibition of works of art of alumnae of Mount Holyoke College, Painting Gallery, Upper Floor. See page 172.

Exhibition of students' work: drawing, Rooms 9 and 11, Upper Floor; modelling, Rooms 3 and 4, Lowest Floor; honor papers, Library, Main Floor.

ASTRONOMY

Physical Laboratory: Room 207

Historical portfolio, "Astronomy in Mount Holyoke's Century." Transparencies: the local group of galaxies; manifestations of solar activity.

John Payson Williston Observatory

In the dome (sky permitting): Venus in crescent phase and the Sun with spots and faculae on view with the telescopes during the day; in the evening, clusters and nebulae, star-transits.

In the lecture room: honor papers, elementary laboratory work, mirror-making, photographs with the Ross camera, early atlases and texts, teaching equipment.

BOTANY

Cornelia Clapp Laboratory: Second Floor, Main Corridor

Guided tour and demonstrations illustrating phases of the history, structure, metabolism, and ecology of the living plant. Exhibits illustrating the development of botanical science.

CHEMISTRY

Shattuck Hall and Cornelia Clapp Laboratory: Rooms 403 and 415

"A Chemistry Class of 1840"; Friday, Shattuck Hall, Room 2.

Exhibit centering about the work of students, past and present, including reprints of alumnae publications, laboratory work of undergraduates and a demonstration of research methods and apparatus used by graduate students. The latter involves a display of types of distilling columns and different instruments for the investigation of optical properties.

CLASSICAL LANGUAGES AND LITERATURES

Williston Memorial Library: Room 39

Exhibit illustrating the history and work of the Department, including representative textbooks in Greek and Latin from 1837 to 1937, theses presented for the degree of Master of Arts, and papers written by honor students. Facsimiles of Greek and Latin manuscripts and early printed editions of classical authors.

ECONOMICS AND SOCIOLOGY

Skinner Hall: Statistical Laboratories D1 and D2

In D1: A statistical analysis in process; demostration of techniques such as the operation of computing machines and the making of charts. Graphic displays.

In D2: Exhibit of laboratory publications, Master of Arts theses and honor papers.

EDUCATION

Skinner Hall: Room B1

Exhibit illustrating contrasts between the schools of Mary Lyon's day and the present, including a series of slides of children's art, a collection of old, new, and foreign texts, blackboard charts, and bulletin board displays.

ENGLISH AND SPEECH

Williston Memorial Library: Room 31

Theses and honor papers; rhyme sheets; major examinations; vocabulary tests; reading lists; freshman literary magazines and examinations; anthologies and other Department publications. Occupational charts of English major students. Compositions illustrating the writing done by Mount Holyoke students.

Skinner Hall: Rooms M1 and M2

Choral speaking demonstration, M1. Voice recording, M2. Speech records will be made, and so far as time allows speech analyses will be given to those who desire them. The cost of the disc is 75 cents.

ENGLISH LITERATURE AND DRAMA
Skinner Hall: Rooms K1 and K3

Exhibit of materials used in literature courses, of students' papers, of programs, including Play and Poetry Shop Talk, sponsored by the Department. Slides illustrating backgrounds of English literature, K1.

Laboratory Theatre, Morgan Road

Presentation of "The Vest Pocket Standby." Tickets must be obtained in advance at the Information Desk, Skinner Hall; seating capacity, 150. Laboratory Theatre open for inspection without tickets, 9–11:30 A.M. Friday.

GEOLOGY AND GEOGRAPHY
*Cornelia Clapp Laboratory: Third and Fourth Floors, Western
Wings and Staircases*

Room 300: Exhibit of drawings, class and laboratory work of students in Physical and Historical Geology. Relief model of vicinity of Mount Toby. Chart showing rise and decline of animal life during the geological history of the earth.

Room 304: Regular museum exhibits.

Room 401: Exhibit of types of maps used in teaching geography; charts and other material used by students in geography. Collection on loan of ancient shoes used in Europe.

Staircases: Collection of foreign dolls and of polished marble specimens.

Williston Memorial Library: Room 104

Sederholm Library of pre-Cambrian geology.

GERMAN LANGUAGE AND LITERATURE
Williston Memorial Library: Room 12

Exhibit illustrating the history and work of the Department, including a display of curious old lesson books and readers contrasted with up-to-date classroom texts.

HISTORY AND POLITICAL SCIENCE
Williston Memorial Library: Rooms 32 and 35

Exhibits showing honors achieved and work done by major and graduate students in the Department, exclusive of printed material forming part of the general exhibit of alumnae publications. Exhibit of seals, such as the Great Seals of England, photostats of English legal documents, and other material used in courses.

HYGIENE AND PHYSICAL EDUCATION HEALTH SERVICE
Cornelia Clapp Laboratory: Rooms 212, 213, 215A

Exhibit showing the history of physical education activities by means of photographs and costumes, the development of visual posture education and physical examinations, mortality and morbidity since the preservation of records, and facilities for and methods of preventive medicine.

MATHEMATICS
Physical Laboratory: Library

Exhibit illustrating the work of the Department, including rare books showing the development of mathematics, models of surfaces, papers submitted by honor students and theses submitted by candidates for the degree of Master of Arts.

MUSIC
Mary Lyon Chapel

Concert by combined college choirs of three hundred voices in a program of works by Dvorak, Bruch, Handel, D'Indy and Clara Tillinghast, including the Centenary anthem. Tickets must be obtained in advance at the Information Desk, Skinner Hall.

PHILOSOPHY AND PSYCHOLOGY
Skinner Hall: Psychological Laboratory, Top Floor

Demonstrations of linguistic and performance tests of intelligence; of tests of musical ability and of color-blindness; of apparatus for measuring speed of reaction and span of attention (tachistoscope); of methods for improving speed and quality of reading. Exhibit of honor papers since 1929.

PHYSICS
Physical Laboratory and Shattuck Hall: Room 3 and Apparatus Room

Exhibit illustrating the history, equipment, and work of the Department with demonstrations of special apparatus.

Third Floor: Museum of early apparatus, and research.

Second Floor: Laboratories for first and second year work and photography.

First Floor: Department Library: exhibit of old books, Master of Arts theses, and senior "special problem" work. Laboratories for standard measurements and electron physics. Foucault pendulum. Apparatus room.

Ground floor: Alternating current and radio laboratory, shop, battery room and research.

Shattuck Hall: General lecture equipment.

PHYSIOLOGY
Cornelia Clapp Laboratory: Third and Fourth Floors, East End

Laboratories: Demonstration of experiments chosen from those usually performed. Laboratory set-ups and results of other experiments.

Room 318: Master of Arts theses, honor papers, student notebooks, faculty publications, pieces of work by graduate students and alumnae. Rare books and recent books. Books and pictures showing physiology in 1837 and in 1937. Various collections showing things the Department works with and enjoys.

HISTORY AND LITERATURE OF RELIGION
Williston Memorial Library: Room 13

Exhibit showing a selection of rare Bibles, of recent books used in various courses, outlines of courses, undergraduate papers, honor and graduate theses, the "Fox Shrine" recently presented to the College, and the achievements of major students in the Department graduating during the last twenty-five years.

ROMANCE LANGUAGES AND LITERATURES
Williston Memorial Library: Rooms 30 and 42

Room 30: Exhibit illustrating the history of the Department and the work done in French, including books, charts, photographs, faculty publications, and student papers and theses.

Room 42: Exhibit illustrating the work done in Italian and Spanish, including honor and other papers, phonograph recording of a play by students of Italian, photographs of social activities, and a chart showing the history of the teaching of Spanish at Mount Holyoke College.

ZOOLOGY
Cornelia Clapp Laboratory: First Floor and Basement

Exhibits illustrating the work of undergraduates, including laboratory, conference and honor courses, and of graduate students. Samples of laboratory reports, honor papers and Master of Arts theses. Demonstrations of typical laboratory work, special techniques, and experiments. Exhibit of moving picture films used in teaching.

DELEGATES FROM COLLEGES, UNIVERSITIES AND SOCIETIES

An asterisk indicates that a delegate who had accepted appointment was finally unable to be present.

DATE OF FOUNDING

XII Century   Oxford University. Dean Katharine McElroy (Wells College)

1303   University of Rome...Professor Gabriella Bosano (Wellesley College)

1636   Harvard University.....................Mr. Jerome Davis Greene

1693   The College of William and Mary in Virginia.....................
Dean Grace Warren Landrum

1701   Yale University.......................Professor Arnold Wolfers

1740   University of Pennsylvania...........Dean Karl Greenwood Miller

1742   Moravian Seminary and College for Women.....................
Professor Mildred Chapman Johnstone

1746   Princeton University.....................Mr. Alexander Leitch

1754   Columbia University...............Dean Virginia C. Gildersleeve

1764   Brown University...........Vice-President James Pickwell Adams

1766   Rutgers University...........*President Robert Clarkson Clothier

1769   Dartmouth College.................Professor John Barker Stearns

1776   Phi Beta Kappa...........Dean Marjorie Nicolson (Smith College)

1780   American Academy of Arts and Sciences....Professor Howard Patch
(Smith College)

1783   Dickinson College..........Professor Nora Mohler (Smith College)

1784   University of the State of New York............Dr. James I. Wyer

1787   University of Pittsburgh.................Professor Ellen M. Geyer

1791   University of Vermont.................Professor Bertha M. Terrill

1793   Williams College.......................President Tyler Dennett

1794   Bowdoin College..................Professor Edward S. Hammond

1795   University of North Carolina...........Professor Francis W. Coker
(Yale University)
Miss Ruth A. Searles

1795   Union College........................President Dixon Ryan Fox

1800   Middlebury College..................Assistant Dean Ruth Temple

1800   University of New Brunswick.............Mrs. Edith M. McNally

1804   Ohio University.......................Mr. Guy D. Miller

1807   Andover Newton Theological School.............................
President Everett Carleton Herrick

1810   American Board of Commissioners for Foreign Missions............
Miss Helen B. Calder

DATE OF
FOUNDING

1812   Hamilton College..............President Frederick Carlos Ferry
1815   Allegheny College..................Professor Edwin Prince Booth
1819   Centre College........................Mrs. Zillah Redd Hopkins
1819   Colgate University...............President George Barton Cutten
1819   University of Virginia........The Reverend Arthur Lee Kinsolving
1820   Colby College........................Dean Ninetta M. Runnals
1821   Amherst College.........................President Stanley King
1821   The George Washington University.........Mrs. Joshua Evans, Jr.
                           Miss Josephine Dwight Mason
1821   McGill University.........Vice-Chancellor Arthur Eustace Morgan
1822   Yale University Divinity School...Professor Clarence Prouty Shedd
1823   Trinity College............................Dr. Irwin Alfred Buell
1824   Franklin Institute of the State of Pennsylvania...................
                         *Mr. Henry Butler Allen
1824   Kenyon College......................President William F. Peirce
1824   Rensselaer Polytechnic Institute.............Miss Harriet R. Peck
1826   Lafayette College.....................Dean Theodore A. Distler
1826   Western Reserve University.........Professor Katherine H. Porter
1827   Lindenwood College........................Professor Alice Parker
1827   University of Toronto...........Professor *Emeritus* Annie L. Laird
        Professor Elizabeth Rebecca Laird (Mount Holyoke College)
1831   Denison University.Professor Kirtley F. Mather (Harvard University)
1831   New York University....................*Mr. Harold O. Voorhis
1831   Wesleyan University.............President James L. McConaughy
1833   Haverford College........Professor *Emeritus* Rufus Matthew Jones
1833   Oberlin College.......................Miss A. Beatrice Doerschuk
1833   University of Zürich.Dr. Hildegard Stücklen (Mount Holyoke College)
1834   Wheaton College......................Dean Miriam F. Carpenter
1835   Marietta College.........................Miss Miriam Manning
1835   Monticello College................President George I. Rohrbough
1836   Alfred University.....................Mrs. Catherine N. Stearns
1836   Union Theological Seminary...........Professor Robert E. Hume
                      Professor Eugene W. Lyman
1836   Victoria University....................Dean Jessie Macpherson
1836   Wesleyan College................*President Dice Robins Anderson
1837   Colby Junior College..................Mr. James Duane Squires
1837   DePauw University......Dean Albert Z. Mann (Springfield College)
1837   Guilford College............................*Mrs. Clyde Milner
1837   Knox College.............................Mr. Edward Caldwell
1837   University of Louisville...............Mrs. Ruth Warner Crawford
1837   University of Michigan.....................*Dean Alice C. Lloyd
1837   Muskingum College.............President Robert M. Montgomery
1839   Massachusetts State Teachers College at Westfield................
                      President Charles Russell

DATE OF
FOUNDING

1840 Massachusetts State Teachers College at Bridgewater..............
                        *President Zenos E. Scott
1841 Queen's University.........................Mrs. James H. Odell
1842 American Oriental Society.......................................
            Professor Mary Inda Hussey (Mount Holyoke College)
1842 Hollins College............................Miss Isabel Hancock
1842 Mary Baldwin College...........*President Lewis Wilson Jarman
1842 Willamette University........................Miss A. Ann Silver
1844 New York State College for Teachers....President A. R. Brubacher
1845 Wittenberg College.........................Mrs. Louis E. Bauer
1846 Beloit College.....................Mr. Elbert Emerson Lochridge
1846 University of Buffalo........................Dr. Janet S. Barnes
1846 Grinnell College....................Mrs. George Meason Whicher
1846 Mount Union College.....................Mrs. Charles R. Keller
1846 Smithsonian Institution................Dr. Charles Greeley Abbot
1847 Carroll College......................Dr. Dorothy Ganfield Fowler
1847 College of the City of New York..*President Frederick B. Robinson
                        Professor Allan P. Ball
1847 Earlham College.......................Dean Halford L. Hoskins
            (Fletcher School of Law and Diplomacy)
1847 Lawrence College..
            Professor Kenneth John Conant (Harvard University)
1847 Otterbein College.......................Dr. Marshall B. Fanning
1847 Rockford College.........Professor Roberta Teale Swartz Chalmers
1847 State University of Iowa....................Mrs. C. W. Eastman
1848 American Association for the Advancement of Science.............
            Dr. Florence R. Sabin (Rockefeller Institute)
1848 Muhlenberg College............Dr. Levering Tyson, President-elect
1848 Williamsport Dickinson Seminary.........*President John W. Long
1848 University of Wisconsin....................Mrs. Robert A. Young
1850 Hiram College.........................Professor Lee E. Cannon
1850 Illinois Wesleyan University........The Reverend Harold D. Suhm
1850 University of Rochester..............Dean Helen Dalton Bragdon
1850 Woman's Medical College of Pennsylvania.....Dean Martha Tracy
1851 Lasell Junior College...............Dean Emeritus Lillie P. Potter
1851 Milwaukee-Downer College...........Professor Frances W. Hadley
1851 Northwestern University...
            Professor Alice W. Mills (Mount Holyoke College)
1851 College of the Pacific..................Dr. Gertrude Sibley Billard
1852 Mills College.................President Aurelia Henry Reinhardt
1853 Frances Shimer Junior College..Professor Emeritus Mary O. Pollard
1853 Washington University...........Professor Cornelia Catlin Coulter
                        (Mount Holyoke College)
1853 Western College.....................President Ralph K. Hickok

1854 Hamline University...................Professor Mary B. Stark
                                (New York Medical College)
1855 Berea College.................Assistant Dean Julia Frances Allen
1855 Elmira College.....................President William S. A. Pott
1855 Pennsylvania State College........Dr. and Mrs. Dugald C. Jackson
1856 Birmingham-Southern College.............Mr. George L. Murtha
1856 Saint Lawrence University.............Mrs. Gertrude Lee Church
1857 Central College......................Dr. Willard Dayton Brown
1857 Lake Forest College....................Miss Rebecca E. Adams
1857 National Education Association..........Miss Mary McSkimmon
1858 Iowa State College..................Professor Adrian H. Lindsey
                                (Massachusetts State College)
1859 Lake Erie College................President Vivian Blanche Small
1859 Whitman College.................Mrs. Gena Branscombe Tenney
1861 Massachusetts Institute of Technology....Professor K. C. Reynolds
1861 Vassar College...............President Henry Noble MacCracken
                                Dean C. Mildred Thompson
1863 Kansas State College....................Miss Rose Louise Child
1863 Massachusetts State College..........President Hugh Potter Baker
1863 National Academy of Sciences...Professor Margaret Floy Washburn
                                (Vassar College)
1864 Bates College.....................President Clifton Daggett Gray
1864 University of Denver............The Reverend Henry L. Wriston
1864 Swarthmore College...................Dean Frances B. Blanshard
1865 Cornell University......................Dr. Mary M. Crawford
1865 Fisk University..........The Reverend William N. DeBerry
1865 University of Kentucky.....................Dr. Sheppard Jones
1865 University of Maine......................Professor Ruth Crosby
1865 Washburn College...........Dean Irene Nye (Connecticut College)
1865 Worcester Polytechnic Institute....Professor George Henry Haynes
1866 American University of Beirut........Mr. Leslie Westbrook Leavitt
1866 University of Chicago Divinity School.Dean *Emeritus* Shailer Mathews
1866 Lebanon Valley College................Miss Mildred Christiansen
1866 University of New Hampshire.........Professor Alfred E. Richards
1866 College of Wooster.......................Miss Winona A. Hughes
1867 Drew University.......................Dean Lynn Harold Hough
                                (Drew Theological Seminary)
1867 University of Illinois...............Professor Lucy Weston Pickett
                                (Mount Holyoke College)
1868 University of California............Professor Leslie Gale Burgevin
                                (Mount Holyoke College)
1868 University of Minnesota.Professor Mary Ellen Chase (Smith College)
1868 Wells College..........................Professor Philena Young
1869 Boston University......................Dean T. Lawrence Davis

DATE OF
FOUNDING

1869   Girton College, Cambridge University..........Dr. Gisela Richter
(Metropolitan Museum, New York)

1869   Pennsylvania College for Women.President Herbert Lincoln Spencer

1869   Purdue University...............President Edward Charles Elliott

1869   Wilson College.......................President Paul Swain Havens

1870   Hunter College of the City of New York.Professor R. Lucille Anderson

1870   The Ohio State University.................Mr. Hurlbut S. Jacoby

1870   Wellesley College...................President Mildred H. McAfee

1871   University of Arkansas...................Mrs. Saunders MacLane

1871   Newnham College, Cambridge University.........................
Mrs. Margery Corbett Ashby

1871   Smith College.....................President William Allan Neilson

1872   Doane College....Professor Fred Rogers Fairchild (Yale University)

1874   Colorado College......Professor Walter Carl Barnes (Smith College)

1874   Huguenot University College...Professor *Emeritus* Florence M. Snell

1874   St. Olaf College..........................Professor Karen Larsen

1875   American College for Girls at Istanbul..Dr. Kathryn Newell Adams

1875   Doshisha University......................Mrs. Toyohiko Takami

1875   Kobe College.............................Miss Masuko Ohtake

1875   Park College.............................Dr. James M. Matthews

1876   American Chemical Society.Professor Evald L. Skau (Trinity College)

1876   American Library Association..............Mr. Hiller C. Wellman

1876   The Johns Hopkins University....Professor Arthur Oncken Lovejoy

1879   Radcliffe College..................President Ada Louise Comstock

1880   The Society of Biblical Literature and Exegesis...................
Professor John W. Flight (Haverford College)

1880   University of Southern California..........Mr. Loring W. Carney

1881   Coe College.......Professor Willa McClung Evans (Hunter College)

1881   Drake University...................The Reverend John Gratton

1881   Spelman College...................President Florence M. Read

1881   Yankton College.....................Mrs. Maud Crawford Gray

1882   American Association of University Women......................
Dr. Kathryn McHale, Director

1883   Huron College.............................Miss Tressa J. Meyer

1884   American Historical Association..........Dr. Mary Hume Maguire
(Radcliffe College)

1884   Mississippi State College for Women........Mrs. Robert H. Russell

1884   Temple University....................President Charles E. Beury

1885   American International College...President Chester Stowe McGown

1885   Bryn Mawr College...............President Marion Edwards Park
Dean Helen Manning

1885   Goucher College.................President David Allan Robertson

1885   New England Association of Colleges and Secondary Schools.......
*Mr. C. Herbert Taylor

1885	Rollins College	Dr. Helen Wieand Cole
1885	Springfield College	Dean Albert Z. Mann
1885	Stanford University	Miss Helen Ella True
1886	Newcomb College	Miss Ruth C. Lawson
1886	Royal Holloway College, University of London	Dr. Caroline Robbins (Bryn Mawr College)
1886	Winthrop College	Miss Annie Caughman
1887	Clark University	Dean Homer P. Little
1887	Columbia University School of Library Service	*Dr. Charles C. Williamson, Director
1887	McMaster University	The Reverend George Arthur Clarke
1887	Pomona College	The Reverend Henry David Gray
1888	American Mathematical Society	Professor Neal Henry McCoy (Smith College)
1888	Columbia University Teachers College	Dr. Helen E. Davis
1888	College of Puget Sound	Professor Samuel Dupertuis (Boston University)
1889	Agnes Scott College	*President James Ross McCain
1889	American Academy of Political and Social Science	Dean Mary Ashby Cheek (Mount Holyoke College)
1889	Barnard College	Dean Virginia C. Gildersleeve
1890	University of Chicago	Professor *Emeritus* Marion Talbot
1890	Yenching University	Mrs. John H. Finley
1891	Drexel Institute of Technology	Dean Ruth A. L. Dorsey Mrs. George C. Gress
1891	Woman's College of the University of North Carolina	Dean W. C. Jackson
1892	American Psychological Association	Professor David Camp Rogers (Smith College)
1892	International Institute for Girls in Spain	Miss Caridad Rodriguez-Castellano
1892	Millsaps College	Mrs. Katie Lou Countiss Pecot
1892	Pembroke College in Brown University	Dean Margaret S. Morriss
1892	Rhode Island State College	Mrs. Alice McCauley
1893	Hood College of Frederick, Maryland	Professor Louise Robinson Heath
1893	Randolph-Macon Woman's College	President Theodore Henley Jack
1893	St. Hilda's College, Oxford University	Dr. Elisabeth Guernsey Kimball (Mount Holyoke College)
1894	Massachusetts State Teachers College at Lowell	*President James Dugan
1894	Massachusetts State Teachers College at North Adams	President Grover C. Bowman
1895	The London School of Economic and Political Science, University of London	Professor Eileen Power

DATE OF
FOUNDING

1895   Massachusetts State Teachers College at Fitchburg...............
                        *President Charles M. Herlihy
1897   Institute of Touraine, University of Poitiers.Professor Hilde K. Held
                        (Mount Holyoke College)
1898   American Astronomical Society.................................
       Professor *Emeritus* Anne Sewell Young (Mount Holyoke College)
                        Dr. Annie J. Cannon (Harvard Observatory)
1899   Simmons College.....................President Bancroft Beatley
1900   American Schools of Oriental Research......Dr. Warren J. Moulton
                        (Bangor Theological Seminary)
1900   Association of American Universities...........................
                        Dean Roland George Dwight Richardson
                        (Graduate School, Brown University)
1900   College Entrance Examination Board.......Dr. Thomas Scott Fiske
1901   James Millikin University..............Miss Grace Patten Conant
1901   Sweet Briar College........................President Meta Glass
1902   International Alliance of Women...President Margery Corbett Ashby
1903   American Political Science Association.President Thomas Reed Powell
1904   College of New Rochelle.....................Mrs. James J. Dowd
1905   Yenching College for Women.................Mrs. John H. Finley
1905   Federal Council of Churches of Christ in America.................
                        The Reverend Samuel McCrae Cavert
1908   William Smith College.....................Mrs. Ralph B. Putney
1910   Jackson College for Women.............Dean Edith Linwood Bush
1911   Reed College.......................Miss Margaret Lenore Wiley
1911   Skidmore College.......................Dean Margaret Bridgman
1912   American Association of Collegiate Registrars..Miss Ella S. Dickinson
                        (Mount Holyoke College)
1914   Westhampton College in the University of Richmond.............
                        Miss Grace Walkins
1915   American Association of University Professors....................
                        Professor Marjorie Williams (Smith College)
1915   Connecticut College....................President Katharine Blunt
1915   Ginling College........Mrs. Lawrence Thurston, President *Emeritus*
1916   National Research Council...........Dean Virginia C. Gildersleeve
                        (Barnard College)
1916   Russell Sage College.............President James Laurence Meader
1916   University of South Africa..................Dr. Florence M. Snell
1918   American Council on Education....President William Allan Neilson
                        (Smith College)
1918   Bartol Research Foundation of the Franklin Institute.............
                        Dr. W. F. G. Swann
1918   New Jersey College for Women....Dean Margaret Trumbull Corwin

EXCHANGE PROFESSORS

Margarete Bieber, Formerly of the University of Giessen, Barnard College

Jan J. L. Duyvendak,* Leyden University, Columbia University

Fritz Heinrich Lewy,* Formerly of the University of Berlin, Hospital of the
    University of Pennsylvania

Hans Rademacher,* Formerly of the University of Breslau, University of
    Pennsylvania

Joachim Wach, Formerly of the University of Leipzig, Brown University

STUDENT DELEGATES FROM DAUGHTER COLLEGES

Mills College. Jane Taylor, '35, former President, Associated Students of
    Mills College

Western College. Edith Drake, President of Student Government

Lake Erie College. Jean Fawcett, President of Student Government

OFFICIAL CLASS REPRESENTATIVES

1861	Emily S. Wilson	1903	Florence Donnell White
1868	Mary Davis Rockwell	1904	Irene Horton Crary
1869	Eleanor Everett Kimball	1905	Helen Bullard Benedict
1872	Mary Ella Spooner Brown	1906	Ella Elizabeth Smith
1873	Clara Herendeen Clark	1907	Elizabeth Briggs Johnson
1874	Lucy Jones Kingsbury	1908	Marion Lewis Cooper
1875	Frances Hazen Gates	1909	Vira Peters Towle
1876	Emma J. Sloan	1910	Mary Preston
1877	Jennie Morehouse Edwards	1911	Helen Crane Weber
1878	Mathilde Ulrich Abercrombie	1912	Christine Everts Greene
1879	Marion Gaylord Atwell	1913	Rebecca Thompson Bell
1880	Helen C. Flint	1914	Sara Cook Wood
1881	Harriet A. McElwain	1915	Cleora Church Doane
1882	Jane E. Doolittle	1916	Alice Dixon Bond
1883	Annie Burnett Hubbard	1917	Margaret E. Conrad
1884	Mary Walker Raymond	1918	Margaret Davis Stitt
1885	Georgiana Hodgkins	1919	Helen Kaan
1886	Harriet R. Pease	1920	Katherine Williams
1887	Kate L. Adams	1921	Mary Louise Forbes Foster
1888	Clara Bliss	1922	Eleanor M. Moore
1889	Mary Ross Harris	1923	Martha Frances David
1890	Mary Louise Allen	1924	Margaret Chickering Bristol
1891	Mary Hadsell Castle	1925	Margaret Walker Carter
1892	M. Helen Keith	1926	Audrey Allen Weech
1893	Olive Sprague Cooper	1927	Erma M. Funk
1894	Edith Hayes Sackett	1928	Lydia R. Kendall
1895	Lydia Sanderson Capen	1929	Margaret Grierson Cole
1896	Florence P. Mowry	1930	Harriette D. Vera
1897	N. Eveline Coolidge	1931	Sidonia Ellis
1898	Lena Aldrich Schuster	1932	Margaret Dunlop Moore
1899	Susan Doane Arnold	1933	Francenia Budd Towle
1900	Estelle Potter Harrison	1934	Ruth M. Timm
1901	Margaret Steen Vauclain	1935	Drue Matthews
1902	Charlotte Leavitt Gilpatric	1936	Dorothea A. Pfeiffer

OFFICIAL CLUB REPRESENTATIVES

BERKSHIRE COUNTY, Edith Hall, '03
BOSTON, Fannie Tower Everts, '12
BRIDGEPORT, Edith Zink Miles, '04
BUFFALO, Emily Rippey Kimber, '21
CENTRAL NEW YORK, Betty Widtman Berg, '20
CENTRAL OHIO, Betsy Farley Jacoby, '10
CHAMPAIGN-URBANA, M. Helen Keith, '92

CHICAGO, Florence Huth, '18
CLEVELAND, Amy F. Rowland, '93
DETROIT, Jennette Thompson Barnes, '20
EASTERN CONNECTICUT, Rena Sweet Vaughan, '86
EASTERN NEW YORK, Clara Springsteed Bacon, '08
FLORIDA, Helen Wieand Cole, '06
FRANKLIN COUNTY, Helen Gaylord Miller, '09
GENESEE VALLEY, Margaret G. Reitz, '29
HAMPSHIRE COUNTY, Bessie N. Leonard, '92
HARTFORD, Marion Moulton Campbell, '04
HOLYOKE, Mary Quirk Williston, '02
HUDSON VALLEY, Marion Viets Rainey, '19
INDIANA, Helen Broeksmit Sinclair, '02
LONG ISLAND, Ellen Wilcox Johnson, '23
MARYLAND, Eunice R. Goddard, '03
MINNESOTA, Louise Sterner Burnett, '03
NEW HAMPSHIRE, Addie E. Towne, '05
NEW HAVEN, Helen Jones Tolles, '05
NEW YORK, Grace Allen Whitney, '17
NORTH CAROLINA, Mary Cummings Bigelow, '17
NORTHERN CALIFORNIA, Letitia Thomas Evans, '95
NORTHERN NEW JERSEY, Nellie Dodd Speers, '12
PHILADELPHIA, Esther L. Jackson, '28
PITTSBURGH, Elizabeth A. Campbell, '18
PUGET SOUND, Harriet H. Smith, '18
RHODE ISLAND, Dorothy Cobb, '26
SCRANTON, Marie Louise Connolly, '07
ST. LOUIS, Eva Grant Barngrove, '89
SOUTHERN CALIFORNIA, Luella Searing Bliss, '14
SPRINGFIELD, Hellen Gay Miller, '04
TRENTON, Alberta Rittenhouse Fuhrmann, '07
VERMONT, Elizabeth Crane Irish, '25
WASHINGTON, D. C., Helen Demond, '25
WATERBURY, Alethea R. Puffer, '03
WESTERN MAINE, Ruby Stockwell Henry, '06
WORCESTER, Etheldred Willmott McKinley, '21

CHINA, Carolyn T. Sewall, '10
INDIA, Katherine Clark Dudley, '14
JAPAN, Harriet Wyckoff Hail, '97

MARSHALS

A. Elizabeth Adams, *Chief Marshal.* Katherine W. Auryansen, Emma P. Carr, Marie Litzinger, Harriet Newhall, Louisa S. Stevenson, Helen MacM. Voorhees.

CENTENNIAL OFFICE AND COMMITTEES

On each committee the chairman is named first.

EXECUTIVE SECRETARY, Marion H. Barbour

OFFICE STAFF. *Secretary for Hospitality*, Mrs. Lawrence C. Wellington; *Secretary*, Mary S. McGonigal; *Assistants*, Jeannette L. Martin, Dorothy E. Welles.

CENTRAL CENTENNIAL COMMITTEE. Dean Edgar S. Furniss (trustee), Dean Harriett M. Allyn, Mr. William H. Baldwin, New York City, Marion H. Barbour, Gertrude V. Bruyn, Boardman Bump, Dean Mary Ashby Cheek, Florence Clement, Caroline B. Greene, William C. Hammond, Marie Heghinian, Amy Hewes, Mary C. J. Higley, Otto C. Kohler, Alva Morrison (trustee), Harriet Newhall, Ada L. F. Snell, Abby H. Turner, Margaret Steen Vauclain (alumna), Maude Titus White (alumna), Louise K. Wilde, President Mary E. Woolley.

EXECUTIVE COMMITTEE. President Mary E. Woolley, Dean Harriett M. Allyn, Marion H. Barbour, Boardman Bump.

ALUMNAE SYMPOSIUM AND LUNCHEONS. Margaret Steen Vauclain, Nell Lothrop Forstall, Mary C. J. Higley, Mary Ely Lyman, Lilla Newkirk Strong, Maude Titus White.

BUILDINGS AND GROUNDS. Otto C. Kohler, Earl Frank, Anders Kjoller.

CENTENARY CEREMONIES. President Mary E. Woolley, Dean Harriett M. Allyn, A. Elizabeth Adams, Margaret Ball, Emma P. Carr, Dean Edgar S. Furniss (trustee), Caroline M. Galt,* William C. Hammond.

CENTENNIAL ARCHIVES. Viola F. Barnes, Mildred S. Howard, John Lobb, Flora B. Ludington Christianna Smith.

CENTENNIAL SCRIBE. Harriet Fox Whicher.

CHECKING WRAPS AND BAGGAGE. Elisabeth G. Kimball, Donald W. Bailey, Ruth J. Dean.

CHRONICLER. Bertha E. Blakely.

DANCE RECITAL. Marie Heghinian, Viola F. Barnes, Laura Yale Churchill (alumna), Robert Ryer.

DEPARTMENTAL EXHIBITS. Abby H. Turner, Charlotte D'Evelyn, Alice H. Farnsworth, Florence W. Foss, Helena M. Gamer, Roger W. Holmes, Ann H. Morgan, Mary L. Sherrill, Jessie M. Tatlock. *Consultants:* Ethel B. Dietrich, Flora B. Ludington.

EMERGENCY. Dr. Pattie J. Groves and Dr. Elizabeth C. Underhill.

EXCURSIONS INTO THE MARY LYON COUNTRY. Kathryn F. Stein, A. Josephine McAmis, Sydney R. McLean, Ruth Sedgwick.

FLOWERS AND PLANTS. Asa S. Kinney, D. J. Connor.

* Died January 17, 1937.

FUND RAISING. Gertrude V. Bruyn, *Field Secretary*, Susan Doane Arnold (alumna), William H. Baldwin, New York City, Boardman Bump, Dean Mary Ashby Cheek, Florence Clement, Paul H. Davis (trustee), Mary C. J. Higley, Henry P. Kendall (trustee), Alva Morrison (trustee), Frank C. Myers (trustee), Harriet Newhall, Maude Titus White (alumna), President Mary E. Woolley, Elizabeth Porter Wyckoff (alumna).

GARDEN PARTY. Dean Harriett M. Allyn. *Costumes:* Louise Wallis and Ethel T. Eltinge, Mrs. Frank E. Bailey, Jr., Mrs. Roger W. Holmes, Mrs. Asa S. Kinney, Mrs. Otto C. Kohler, Mrs. Rogers D. Rusk, Nancy M. Eggleston, 1938, Elizabeth McN. Main, 1937. *Historical Pantomime:* Helen P. Wheeler, Mrs. Dean N. Currie, Sydney R. McLean, Dorothy B. Jackson, 1937, Katharine E. Metcalf, 1937, Alice N. Wiley, 1938. *Reception:* Blanche E. Brotherton and Constance Meadnis Saintonge. *Grounds:* Otto C. Kohler. *Music:* William C. Hammond.

HONORARY DEGREES—FACULTY COMMITTEE. Caroline M. Galt,* Emma P. Carr, Ann H. Morgan, N. Neilson, Ada L. F. Snell, Stuart M. Stoke.

HONORARY DEGREES—TRUSTEE COMMITTEE. Florence Purington, Dr. William H. Day, Helene Pope Whitman.

HOSPITALITY. Dean Mary Ashby Cheek. *Chairman for Alumnae Hospitality,* Mary C. J. Higley. *Secretary for Hospitality,* Mrs. Lawrence C. Wellington. *Holyoke:* Mrs. Edward N. White and Dorothy Broas McDowell, Ruth Hubbard Heidner, Fern Wheeler Judd, Helen Chapin Read, Louise Reynolds Weiser. *Amherst:* Elizabeth Ball Cowan, Sarah Hartman Jones, Mary Fitzgerald McKeon, Susan Reed Stifler. *Northampton:* Grace Moore Heider, Clara P. Bodman, Bessie N. Leonard, Virginia Greene Richards. *Springfield:* Dorothy S. Adams and Mildred Welch Skipton, Mabel Rice Bacon, May Fiske Beatty, Eunice B. Burbank, Jessie Caton Carman, Alice S. Halligan, Hellen Gay Miller, Mary Bruyn Quimby, Meta Mallary Seaman, Mary Cheney Stephenson, Adeline Johnson Sweet. *South Hadley:* Mary K. Beard, Florence Adams, Mrs. Dwight Bloodgood, Myra Platt Bracewell, Bessie Gridley Canney, Esther Judge Fay, Mrs. Charles Hayes, Helen Blythe Hazen, Amy Stone Judge, Mrs. Earl B. MacMillan, Mary L. Sherrill, Edith Palmer Towne, Helen Wheeler, Adeline Stockwell Winchester. *Campus: Rooms for Guests,* Doris E. Hutchinson, *Household Arrangements,* Alice McCool, *Meals in Campus Houses,* Olive Niles.

INFORMATION CENTER. Mary S. McGonigal, Helen E. Freeman, Jeannette L. Martin, Dorothy E. Welles.

INTELLECTUAL CONTRIBUTIONS. Ethel B. Dietrich, A. Elizabeth Adams, Florence Clement (Secretary), Caroline M. Galt,* Elizabeth R. Laird, Flora B. Ludington, Bertha H. Putnam, Christianna Smith, Ada L. F. Snell.

* Died January 17, 1937.

REGISTER OF THE FACULTY OF MOUNT HOLYOKE COLLEGE. Christianna Smith, Alice Carver Cramer, Ruth J. Dean, John Lobb, Marion Marsh Randall, Kathryn F. Stein, Edward C. Weist.

INVITATIONS. Caroline B. Greene, Katherine W. Auryansen, Mary L. Sherrill, Ellen B. Talbot.

LUNCHEON FOR GUESTS. Grace M. Bacon, Mary L. Sherrill and M. Louise Jewett, Anne W. Bolton, Marie Litzinger.

MAIL FOR GUESTS. Charlotte Haywood, Frances E. Baker.

MUSIC. William C. Hammond, Ruth E. Douglass, Clara B. Tillinghast, Viva F. Richardson.

PREPARATION OF THE CAMPUS AND GENERAL DÉCOR. Amy Hewes, Florence W. Foss, Otto C. Kohler, Hildegarde Snow (alumna), Margaret P. Surré, Boston.

PRINTING. Florence Clement.

PUBLICATIONS. Ada L. F. Snell, Viola F. Barnes, Emma P. Carr.

DISPLAY AND SALE OF PUBLICATIONS. Erika M. Meyer, Helena M. Gamer.

PUBLICITY. Louise K. Wilde, Sylvia Smyth Hawkins, Martha E. Kelley, Rosemary Wardle.

RECEPTION TO GUESTS. Mary K. Beard and Alice R. Dresser, Alice McCool, Andrew Vitali.

REGISTRATION OF GUESTS. Harriet J. Eustis, Marion Sanderson Davis, Dorothy P. Day, Harriet Newhall, Mrs. Lawrence C. Wellington.

ROOM ASSIGNMENTS (*In academic buildings*). Doris E. Hutchinson, Louise S. Graham.

SERENADE AND CANOE PAGEANT. Katharine R. Swenarton, 1937, R. Ruth Baird, Ruth E. Douglass, Elizabeth P. Clark, 1940, Dorothy L. Fuller, 1939, Dorothy O. Grumpelt, 1940, Mildred S. Howard, Louise H. Johnson, 1940, Ann MacMillan, 1940, Ruth E. Matthews, 1939, Ella Way, 1940, Judith B. Welles, 1938.

SERVICE OF COMMEMORATION. David E. Adams, Ruth E. Douglass, William C. Hammond, Dorothy L. Mills, 1937, Helen MacM. Voorhees.

STUDENT CENTRAL CENTENNIAL COMMITTEE. Sarah B. Cole, 1937, Anne M. Calder, 1938, Helen A. Chapman, 1937, Dean Mary Ashby Cheek, Barbara A. Davis, 1937, Ruth F. Friedson, 1937, Dean Hosken, 1940, Jane W. Hume, 1937, H. Virginia Hunter, 1937, Dorothy B. Jackson, 1937, Lois E. Krieger, 1938, C. Maud H. Lynch, Elizabeth McN. Main, 1937, Marianna McNees, 1937, Dorothy L. Mills, 1937, Mary Alice Myers, 1937, Carolyn C. Raye, 1937, Elizabeth O. Stavers, 1937, Katharine R. Swenarton, 1937, Mary E. Tuttle, 1937, Ethel R. Williamson, 1939.

STUDENT FROLIC. Mary E. Tuttle, 1937, Janet Arbuckle, 1937, Dean Mary Ashby Cheek, Dean Hosken, 1940, Dorothy B. Jackson, 1937, Kathro Kidwell, Elizabeth O. Stavers, 1937, Katharine R. Swenarton, 1937.

HISTORIES OF STUDENT ORGANIZATIONS. Jane W. Hume, 1937, Sarah B. Cole, 1937, Barbara A. Davis, 1937, Dorothy B. Jackson, 1937, C. Maud H. Lynch, Marianna McNees, 1937, Mary Alice Myers, 1937, Elizabeth O. Stavers, 1937, Katharine R. Swenarton, 1937, Mary E. Tuttle, 1937. *Authors of Organization Histories:* Mary B. Byers, 1938, Llamarada; M. Ellen Dix, 1938, Glee Club; Dorothy B. Jackson, 1937, and Mary J. Smith, 1937, Dramatic Club; Dorothy H. Knapp, 1939, Athletic Association; Lois E. Krieger, 1938, Mount Holyoke News; Marianna McNees, 1937, Social Life; Jean L. Stout, 1939, Fellowship of Faiths.

STUDENT SERVICE. Helen MacM. Voorhees, Katherine W. Auryansen, E. Virginia Brillinger, Gertrude Evans, Henrietta T. Hall, Drue E. Matthews.

TICKETS. D. Helen Wolcott, Elizabeth Coster, Margaret M. Endicott, Ruth M. Morrison, Julia M. Shipman.

TRANSPORATION. Ruth M. Morrison, Elaine D. McCollum, 1937, Frances Powers, Springfield, Mrs. H. B. Wickersham, Holyoke.